RETOOLING
ON THE RUN

RETOOLING ON THE RUN ·

Real Change for Leaders With No Time

Stuart Heller

David Sheppard Surrenda

Frog, Ltd.
Berkeley, California

Published by Frog, Ltd.

Frog, Ltd. books are distributed by
North Atlantic Books
P.O. Box 12327
Berkeley, California 94712

Cover and book design by Paula Morrison
Typeset by Catherine Campaigne

Printed in the United States of America by Malloy Lithographing

Library of Congress Cataloging-in-Publication Data

Surrenda, David.
   Retooling on the run : real change for leaders with no time / David Surrenda, Stuart Heller.
       p.   c.m.
   Includes bibliographical references.
   ISBN 1–883319–19–6 (pbk.)
      1. Organizational change—Management 2. Leadership—Psychological aspects. 3. Strategic planning. 4. Executives—Psychology. I. Heller, Stuart, 1947– . II. Title.
   HD58.8.S87   1994
   658.4′092—dc20   93–40411
                                                                        CIP

1   2   3   4   5   6   7   8   9   /   98   97   96   95   94

ACKNOWLEDGMENTS

I dedicate this book to my loving, wise, and incredibly patient wife, Carol.
SH

This book is dedicated to my daughters—Jennifer, Leah, and Rhiannon—who embody the spirit of this book and for my fathers whose inspirations gifted me in rich and vastly different ways.
DSS

Our quality of life depends on the quality of our leaders.
It's up to you.

If you've ever had dreams of leadership,
this is the time,
this is the place
and you're it.

—Warren Bennis

TABLE OF CONTENTS

"YOU ARE THE first organization you must master" was the seed idea from which this book grew. It was clear to us that instituting social or corporate change could never succeed without a corresponding effort by leaders to cultivate personal mastery. This idea has become increasingly apparent to those interested in developing learning organizations.

The organizations that we seek to change were built by people. To make real changes in the way our companies work we have to face the many paradoxes that make us human. If we are to succeed, we have to integrate the apparently opposite domains of head and heart, power and compassion, profit and service, and personal and professional.

Over the course of the years we invested in the development of this book, we maintained our focus on one key issue — the relationship between the mastery of self and the mastery of work, or in other words, between the internal and external dimensions of life.

Finding the time to work on this issue in the midst of our already full schedules is the first major challenge. In the face of this, most people choose to focus their attention on work over self. The traditional methods for indepth personal retooling require you to take off significant time, stop your current work, and perhaps even leave your home to devote yourself to study.

We used the concept of "no time" to point to another way to approach this dilemma. No time does not mean instant change or quick fixes. Cultivating personal mastery and more versatile habits when you cannot stop your life to study requires the employment of a strategy that uses your everyday life as the training ground. It necessitates a relatively small investment of time and energy upfront to learn a set of practices (internal actions) that you can use at the same time you are involved with your daily responsibilities. As you simultaneously complete your work and retool yourself, you are truly leveraging your time.

Stuart brought to this project his many years of study of the martial arts and movement psychology. David spent those same years leading, growing, and building organizations. What we had in common was the tendency to ask deep and difficult questions that penetrated conventional wisdom. We originally called this project, *The Executive Warrior* — an image of creativity, action, and courage. We wanted to bring together the warrior's body-based skill with the executive's vision and leadership skills.

Despite our radically different paths and temperaments — Stuart was near-sighted and David was far-sighted; David wanted to write a timely book, and Stuart wanted a timeless one — we found that we agreed on all the fundamentals.

Real change demands an open-ended process. We tried to create a foundation for learning that encourages a fresh look at the complex issues that surround intentional change. We offer it in the hope that you can use it to empower your journey of accomplishment.

INTRODUCTION

WE ARE ALL facing tremendous changes in our work and personal lives. Pressures from work, family, friends, and personal health draw upon our precious available hours. Time is a big issue. Life has speeded up for most people and is not likely to slow down in the foreseeable future. It is easy to see how self-development can take a back seat to daily survival.

This book begins with the premise that significant personal growth and professional development can be attained even with our busy lives and rigorous work schedules. At home, at work, and in our communities, we can turn the tests we face into opportunities for learning. We can and must grow in response to life's challenges.

Change is not easy. If it was, all of the books, seminars, and tapes would have helped us long ago. Change is confusing, frightening, and frustrating. We often end up with more questions and questionable results.

- What and how much should I change?

- How much time and energy will it take?

- Is it really possible and do I really have to?

We all want what works, what lasts, and what is real or authentic. We have had enough of the fads and shortcuts that have gained meteoric attention and then disappeared. We are also tired of struggling to change. We don't have to live out the myth of Sisyphus, who endlessly rolled the rock uphill, only to have it fall all the way back to the beginning.

Retooling on the Run is about self-discovery and developing the inner authority to guide your own change process consistent with your personal and professional goals. We provide the starter-kit of concepts and exercises and by using them you can take a measurable, concrete step forward. The book focuses on the processes of learning, change, and achievement.

Retooling is the process of reconstructing an organization's basic mode of operating. This process requires a serious and ongoing engagement with the infrastructure and its habits of action. This is as possible for an individual as it is for a corporation. In other words, we can retool ourselves. The on-the-run component of our strategy takes into account the relentless issue of "no time." This means that you do not have to relinquish critical work time to devote to pure study. By exploring both *what* you do and *how* you do it, you can leverage your investment of time and energy.

Our retooling-on-the-run strategy also emphasizes the importance of cultivating versatility. This is the ability to shift your style, behavior, or state of mind to fit the situation. When it is time to be expressive, caring, analytical, or in control, you can do it. By training for increased versatility, you build the capacity to respond, and not just react, to challenge. In a time of accelerated change, when we are being continually called upon to invent new solutions, versatility is a necessity and not a luxury.

Working with versatility stretches your repertoire of perception, action, and choice. This counterbalances the natural tendency to choose that which is familiar and comfortable. For example, someone who is used to being in control will even attempt to control their efforts at being spontaneous. By increasing your options for action, it becomes possible to resist the siren's pull of habit and make new choices in your life.

Versatility is most effectively learned with a whole body approach. Your words are not the only source of your meaning. You telegraph your attitudes and beliefs with every inflection, gesture, and movement. You think, feel, move, communicate, interact, and imagine with your body. What you learn when you use your whole body directly transfers to your daily life.

Working with versatility strengthens your capacity to act as a unified and coordinated whole. Integrating your whole body into the learning process can bring both awareness and power to your actions. This leads to a different and more positive quality of experience.

We are living in the time of the parenthesis, the time between eras. Those who are willing to handle the ambiguity of this in between period and to anticipate the new era will be a quantum leap ahead of those who hold onto the past. The time of the parenthesis is a time of change and questioning.

Although the time between eras is uncertain, it is a great and yeasty time, filled with opportunity. If we can learn to make uncertainty our friend, we can achieve much more than in stable eras.

—John Naisbitt

A NEW FOUNDATION
FOR LEADERSHIP

1

CHANGING YOURSELF TO CHANGE YOUR ORGANIZATION

Only those who constantly retool themselves stand a chance of staying employed in the years ahead.

—Tom Peters

IN A SMALL town, a young piano player had a dream. Considered to be a child prodigy, his goal was to become an internationally renowned pianist. Far surpassing his first teachers, he contemplated travelling to New York to fulfill his dream of studying with a master teacher.

Finally his chance appeared. He was invited to audition with one of the most renowned teachers in the world. Under the master's knowing gaze he drew forth his best performance. Afterwards he spoke of his dream of becoming a true virtuoso.

The maestro contemplated what he had just heard and said, "The goal that you wish to achieve is possible, but I do not know if you are prepared to do what it will take. Your performance was excellent. However, your method has very severe limits. You have achieved more with it than I would have expected. The real problem is that the method you are using is not the method of a true virtuoso. It cannot take you to the heights you wish to attain. You have already gone far beyond the limits of your current technique. The path to virtuosity begins by returning to the basics of piano technique in order to reconstruct a method that has open-ended potential.

"Travelling the path I see before you is very difficult. Consciously going back to the beginning is more challenging than you imagine. The

3

issue here is more than physical technique alone. You are the real instrument that must be mastered. All of you is presented in how you play. If you are to be a master, you must learn to face your fears and wrestle with your habits. When you are able to do this successfully, you will be ready to reach within yourself to bring forth your genius."

Whether we realize it or not, we are constantly facing the same question that the pianist faces. However, we have the additional difficulty of not having enough time. Caught up in our busy, day-to-day existence, we long for the opportunity to further develop our abilities. Realizing our dreams of service and success is critical to our sense of purpose and self-esteem. However, the pace of modern life allows few breathing spaces for such self-development.

Constantly facing the pressure to make things happen now, we struggle with how to improve ourselves without having the time to do it. Living in this environment of stress and overwork, we find ourselves drawn to the quick fix methods. We have all heard the story of the ten easy lessons that will make you an expert, the claims that you can learn a foreign language in two weeks, cook like a French chef in a week, receive enlightenment in a weekend, or make a million dollars without doing anything.

We know these claims are false, but we wish they were true nonetheless. We hope that a simple and easy technique will reduce our immediate discomfort. However, time usually shows the ineffectiveness and negative side effects of this Band-Aid approach. As a result, we have become cynical about shortcuts because so few real ones exist.

GOING BACK TO THE BEGINNING

The maestro states that the only way to develop the playing habits of a top pianist is to return to the beginning learning state by letting go of the old habits that interfere with the possibility of becoming a virtuoso. This is the prerequisite for adding on a new technique.

The maestro knows that the simple addition of new technique is unworkable. It is a quick fix approach. His method of returning to the beginning by letting go of the old habits is the essence of the process of retooling.

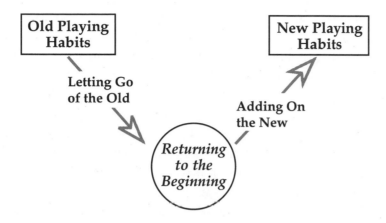

Figure 1–1.

Jack Nicklaus, one of the great golfers of all time, has described his method as follows. Whenever his game goes "bad," he returns to his hometown and his original teacher and tears apart his whole game. He goes back to the basics, again and again. He looks for hidden weaknesses or behavior patterns that may distort his performance. He knows he has to consciously return to the beginning in order to refine and rebuild his game. He chooses this even though he knows that he has to pass through a period of seeming inadequacy and fear.

Companies have to go through a similar process. In order to compete, they have to periodically change or improve their products. Changing the mechanics of the current manufacturing production line is called retooling. Its purpose is to update the system technology. The changeover begins by stopping the wheels of production. The equipment that is no longer needed is then replaced by new technology.

The changeover begins by stopping the wheels of production. The equipment that is no longer needed is replaced and that which can still be used is adjusted. In addition, there is the human issue of which employee skills are no longer needed, which skills must be added, and who can be retrained. This process doesn't happen overnight. Typically, productivity is reduced to zero during the rebuilding.

In personal retooling, when you consider letting go of your old strategies, uncertainty, discomfort, and apprehension arise. The old is comfortable and familiar. Naturally, you are attached to your patterns, believing that they will still work in the future. Once the success grooves are created, they become the path of least resistance. This situation is unavoidable. Your habits would rather have a familiar solution than a new method. It is easy to imagine having the desire to change your unsuccessful action habits. It is another matter to face letting go of the actions that have brought you success in the past. So it is important to consciously ask yourself, *would you rather have your old style of "limited" success, or would you rather have open-ended potential?*

Growth requires risk. Risk requires courage. Courage is the strength to step into the uncertain waters of change. The closer you get to the heart of yourself, the more you realize that what stops you is not outside you. It is within you.

The greater your success, the more you realize that you do not need external opponents. The real battle is with the old action habits that keep you locked into your behavior patterns. The new game of achievement begins by recognizing how *you* are in your own way. The challenge now becomes to get out of the way and into the flow of powerful action. The satisfaction that derives from self-mastery is far greater than any other victory.

The beginning state of learning is analogous to the neutral gear of a stick shift transmission. You cannot shift from one gear to another without passing through neutral. In this beginner's state, there is an

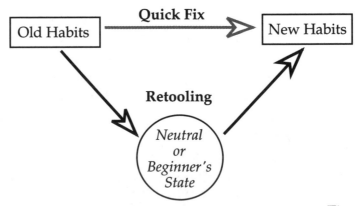

Figure 1–2.

openness to learning, a spontaneity of action, and an opportunity to repattern your habits. Cultivating neutral is at the heart of retooling-on-the-run.

Retooling-on-the-run is a method for achieving deep change while continuing in the normal context of life. Life is the gymnasium where you "work out" and develop new awareness and capacity. By integrating this learning strategy into your daily responsibilities, you can radically reduce the time it takes to acquire positive, new habits.

Historically, two different kinds of results have been sought through personal retooling: 1. **specific behavioral skills** and 2. **versatility of response.**

The first approach develops a new set of discrete skills. For example, a manager who is transferred from being in charge of Telecommunications to directing Warehouse Operations has to learn new, specific skills to manage her new role. Another example is the right-handed baseball player who trains to "pull the ball" to left field, no matter where the pitcher throws it, in order to get more batting power and run production.

The second approach focuses on developing versatility in action. To retool for versatility is quite different than training for a specific behavioral goal. Versatility is the ability to use a variety of action styles. For example, imagine a situation to which there are multiple responses. Each of us has a tendency to repeatedly choose one action over any of the others. This pattern, played out over a period of time, becomes our historical style or way of operating. This is our **action bias.**

Versatility is the ability to respond with a full option matrix of behaviors. For example, to continue with the baseball batting analogy, the player retooled for versatility learns to "go with the pitch" and hit to all fields. Unlike the previous example where the batter just focused on learning to pull the ball, in this example, pulling the ball is one of many options that might be chosen. Depending on circumstances, desire and intention, the versatile batter might elect any of the possibilities.

To enhance versatility, it is usually suggested that you add on missing characteristics. Contrary to conventional wisdom, we contend this is a quick fix which does not work. Taking on a new behavior does work briefly but does not yield a sustainable shift in operating habits. This new behavior gets layered on top of all of your old habits. Under stress, there is a strong tendency to revert to older habits. This is an example of the principle, "the last learned is the first lost." Every additional layer of habit takes us further from the neutral gear or beginner's mind of authenticity.

The gear shift analogy can also be applied to the concept of versatility. We must return to neutral, the open learning state where we can release our prior habits and tendencies. The strategy of retooling-on-the-run employs the practice of shifting from one style to another by consciously passing through neutral. Training this way employs the same idea as the maestro's injunction to the piano student: return to the beginning. To achieve versatility, we must become beginners again, examining the structures and dynamics of our patterns of thinking, feeling and moving.

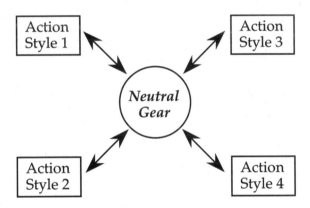

Figure 1–3.

Personal retooling is about cultivating the new habits that correspond to our vision of the future. This task is more difficult than we imagine because what we wish to change is intimately connected to our way of being. Our old identities are inseparable from our habits of action.

We have been culturally trained to compartmentalize ourselves and to value some parts over others. We have been conditioned to pay more attention to *what* we do than to *how* we do it. We have developed the habit of being run by our habits.

In order to arrive at what you do not know, you must go by the way which is the way of ignorance.

—T. S. Eliot

THE NATURE OF CHANGE

The skill to make changes and the sensitivity to recognize when it is the time to do so is more important than ever. We are living in a time of escalating changes. National boundaries are changing. Political systems are changing. The ways we do business are changing. All these changes are directly impacting our lives. We are facing more changes, and ones of greater magnitude, than at any time in human history. The changes required of us in the future may not be like any in the past.

Change is not a human invention. Change is the nature of the world. In its wake are found movement, stress and conflict. No matter how long something has existed, it is still subject to the three action-principles of change

- *creation:* something new arises

- *preservation:* it stays for a period of time

- *destruction:* it then disappears

These principles are found in every system, human as well as corporate. Therefore, it is important to make friends with change. How we understand and react to change influences our lives on every level. When change is perceived as a threat, it is natural to resist by holding on to what we have for fear of what will come. This is an overemphasis on the preservation phase in the belief that staying the same has nothing to do with change.

We sometimes realize that our way of operating does not work as well as it once did. However, given our propensity to resist change, we tend to overcontrol and dream of magical solutions to our problems. The most challenging issues we face cannot be solved with our old personal patterns of action. To make an enduring change, the fundamental habits of the system must change. Lasting change can be the natural side effect of a new, more versatile way of perceiving, acting, and responding.

Authentic, sustainable change cannot be generated by working with the surface layers of behavior and experience. We must learn to reach below the obvious issues to the internal patterns upon which the outer structures are built. When you access this foundation, you can make a real difference in your life.

This is precisely what the retooling strategy is designed to do. Within the context of your daily life, you can begin to reorganize your habits and behaviors. The strategy works by helping you consciously dismantle your old habits. The stumbling blocks to future success are your unrecognized patterns of self-organization.

Experience has shown that by strategically disturbing the complacency of your habits, the development of your action awareness can be fostered. With this awareness, it becomes much easier to recognize the new actions that you need to take and to organize yourself to accomplish them.

The secret to the strategy is wholeness-in-action. By being in touch with the whole of a situation (including yourself, your team and your environment), you can choose and act with wisdom. Most poor decisions and actions come from failure to grasp the full scope of the situation. Too often decisions are made from partial perspectives, without a full grasp of the implications for the individuals or the system.

To make a change in any part of you, you have to change all of you. There is no way around this. Any strategy that suggests you can just change a part of you ignores your fundamental wholeness. It pretends the parts are not connected.

The path of accomplishment is built upon action. Your visions cannot be achieved without it. There are two sides to action and both are critical to success: *what I do* and *how I do it*.

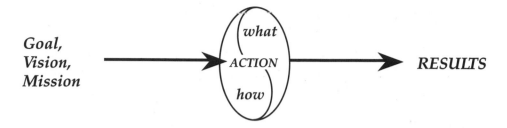

Figure 1–4.

SECOND-ORDER CHANGE

The significant problems we face cannot be solved at the same level of thinking we were at when we created them.

—Albert Einstein

The maestro presented the piano student with the possibility of making a profound change. In the language of mathematics, this is referred to as the difference between first-order and second-order change.

For the piano student, a first-order change would be to further improve his fundamentally flawed method. A second-order change would be to retool his basic technique and his approach to the instrument and to himself. Vital to that retooling are the three action-principles of change (creation, preservation, and destruction). To accomplish his goals, the student would have to *let go* of whatever part of his technique was now recognized as inadequate, he would have to identify and *keep* that which was still effective, and he would have to *add on* that which would allow him to fulfill his potential.

If we use the example of a board game such as checkers, then first-order change is like moving the pieces to different places on the board. As the old saying goes, the more things change the more they remain the same. No matter how you move the pieces, they are still on the same board.

Second-order change alters the board on which you are playing. It is a change at the level of the whole and that shifts everything. New moves become possible and certain old moves become more difficult, if not impossible. This order of change cuts to the core of how you perceive and act.

For personal retooling, second-order change requires an awareness of the relationships between your muscles and your mind. Without muscles, there is no action. If your muscles don't change along with your ideas, you only have first-order change. Your muscles are like the playing field or chess board in the analogy above. Changing the way you use your muscles, as well as your mind, is essential to second-order change. It takes courage to choose and pursue deep change, when you have already achieved a level of success in your life.

James

James, a project director in a science-based company, requested help. He had developed a negative reputation for being insensitive to the responses and concerns of others. He used the "fact" of heavy workloads and deadline pressures to justify his lack of people skills. He acknowledged that he literally sprinted from office to office, dropping things on people's desks, hurriedly giving instructions, and racing on to the next task. He was unwilling to stop for questions or listen to complaints. When he overheard a conversation in which he was described as being one of the most difficult people to work with, he decided he had to do something about it.

In order to give him a new platform for investigation, he was first taught the Centered Presence exercise that you will learn later in this section. By expanding his attention to include his entire body, he was able to notice, for the first time, that he held a great deal of tension in his jaw. As he continued to explore this, he discovered that every time he was in his habitual driven and insensitive mode, his jaw was almost wired shut.

Every time he was able to relax the tight jaw muscles, even if just for a moment, everything felt different. His vision was no longer collapsed into a long, tight tunnel. All of a sudden he could pay attention to what was going on around him. When he was in this muscular state, it wasn't a big deal to stop and listen. The minute he got caught up in his habit of squeezing his jaw tight, the pressure would seem to grow and he would immediately return to pushing through people as though they were the problem. When he again relaxed his jaw, he slowed down and began to interact with people, objects, and all incoming stimuli in a new way.

James reported that the simple act of relaxing his jaw muscles radically changed his perceptions and thoughts. He told us, "I feel like a new person. I've always known that I could be like this, but I didn't know how to change my actions and make it happen."

For years he had been trying to change this behavior pattern. He would have a new insight and then change, for just a short time. He realized that all of his efforts had been focused on changing his mind. When his muscles were added to the equation, he was able to observe, for the first time, how his behavior was triggered. With this new awareness, he found himself able to stop the pattern and instead substitute a relaxation response.

> *For every thought supported by feeling, there is a muscle change. Man's whole body records his emotional thinking.*
> —Mabel Ellsworth Todd, *The Thinking Body*

Vic Braden, founder of a successful tennis college, has spent years interviewing and videotaping the top athletes from a variety of sports. Using stop-action, single-frame videotape, he was able to analyze, in detail, the actual mechanics of their skills. His most striking finding is that no one actually does what they think they are doing. Specifically, if they report that they are swinging their golf club or tennis racket a particular way, the videotape reveals that their perceptions were not matched by their actions. Even the most sophisticated and expert players had difficulty reporting their actual mechanics. We need to become astute observers of our action patterns, if we are going to change them.

> *Many people are caught in the trap of unconscious habit. They cannot escape because they do not perceive what they are doing, as they are doing it.*
> —Frank Pierce Jones, *Body Awareness in Action*

The only pathway to true mastery is through the realm of learning. The only thing that can stop us is our fear of loss and change. The following illustration points to the well-known relationship between perceived risk and fear. Subjectively, as our experience of risk grows, there is a natural increase in our sense of fear. Consistent with our childhood programming that we "shouldn't be afraid" and our adult desire not to experience the discomfort of anxiety, many people retreat into the comfort zone by reducing the amount of risk they take.

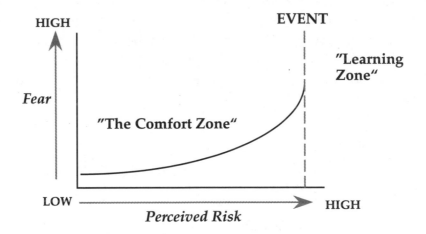

Figure 1–5.

The dilemma is that learning, growth, and change all exist in the areas that are associated with perceived vulnerability and risk. It is the role and responsibility of the leader to take on this challenge. If we are to achieve the gifts of the learning zone, then we must actively climb the fear/risk curve by acknowledging our anxiety reactions but continuing to relax (as much as possible) in the face of the fear. This is accomplished by training ourselves to perceive the fear as a natural by-product of increased risk. Fear need not be a deterrent to action. We have the capacity to continue to act appropriately despite the bodily reactions that might stop us.

In psychological research conducted on both novice and experienced parachutists, psychologists measured the time and intensity of anxiety prior to jumping.[1] The research revealed that novice jumpers experienced the greatest degree of anxiety immediately prior to the jump. Experienced jumpers showed a very different pattern of reaction. While they experienced a rise in their level of excitation/anxiety, it was significantly prior to the event. Immediately before the jump they experienced a decrease in their anxiety and expressed it as a sense of energy and excitement. It is clear that the repeated exposure to an experience can lead to reduction in the perceived sense of risk and consequently the experience of fear.

> *Action absorbs anxiety.*
> —Hans Selye, *The Stress of Life*

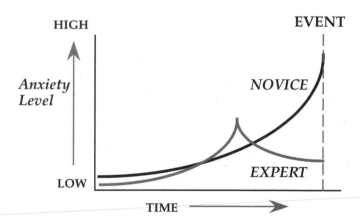

Figure 1–6.

To achieve our goals, we must continue to expose ourselves to the "risks" associated with learning and change. As Babe Ruth, the Yankee home-run slugger said, "Never let the fear of striking out get in your way."

CLARIFYING YOUR GOALS

Each of us is a work-in-progress with different goals and a distinctive personal process. If you are passionately interested in becoming the person you know you can be, then it is vital to question both your goals and your methods. When your goal is not clear and you are not using the appropriate method, achieving your results will be difficult.

It is important to stop periodically and see where you are relative to your goals. Consider the following questions

- What do I want to learn and become?

- What behaviors or qualities do I want more of or less of?

- How do I want others to respond to me?

- How will I know when I have changed?

- Where am I now in relation to my goals?

- How do I get in my own way?

- What am I willing to do to achieve my goals?

These basic questions and your answers act as an anchor as you move through the experiments that make up the core of this book. Our intention is to support the unfolding of your path of discovery and accomplishment.

THE VERSATILE LEADER

Any time we are faced with a decision that impacts others, we are in the realm of the leader. It is not just a position on a organization chart but a way of acting. Anyone, whether they are a manager or a member of a team can step up to the plate and be a leader.

There is a commonly recognized crisis in leadership. We need to find, develop, and train leaders who are capable of responding to the complexity of events which appear as the unsolvable problems we collectively face. These problems threaten our survival as a species.

Developing our personal leadership skills to the fullest is an essential step towards a safe and prosperous future. Peter Drucker observed that "managers had better assume that the skills, knowledge, and tools they will have to master and apply fifteen years hence are going to be different and new, and only they, themselves, can take responsibility for the necessary learning and for directing themselves." We need leaders who know that they are the lever for breakthrough.

Leaders who have the wisdom and compassion to navigate such a challenging time are needed now more than ever. One of the most important traits of a leader is the ability to be versatile in response to difficult situations. One circumstance might call for being receptive, the next for being aggressive, a third might demand structured decisions, and a fourth situation might ask for flexible responses.

You are the first organization you must master. No one can do this for you. It is your responsibility. Your results are a function of the way you organize and use yourself. By studying your patterns of reaction, belief, tension, feelings, and posture, you learn how you both hinder and help yourself.

To study yourself is to study change.

To change your organization, it is necessary to learn how to change yourself. This can be accomplished by training the body and mind together, instead of separately. In this way, you can develop habits that encourage the emergence of versatility.

> *If you teach an individual first to be aware of his physical organism and then to use it as it was meant to be used, you can often change his entire attitude to life.*
>
> —Aldous Huxley

2

BUILDING A FOUNDATION FOR SECOND-ORDER CHANGE

People, like nations, are prone to pitch their tent at the first summit conquered.

—Pierre Teilhard de Chardin

CHANGE IS THE process of shifting from one way of being and acting to another. We begin with the present "you" and end with the future "you." Most experts agree about the necessity of having a new vision or a clear set of goals to assist the change process. Typically, we are advised to reprogram our mind to fit our conscious goals or desires. Some teachers suggest that this can be accomplished by repeating, over and over, new conversations and behaviors. This cognitive method does work, to a degree. However, it does not go deep enough. The power of the old habits cannot be unwound using only the mind.

Despite your dedicated motivation to change, you will encounter your system's inherent resistance to change. This resistance may show up right at the beginning or it may "wait" until you are sure that you have changed and have relaxed your vigilance. Confident that you have changed, you discover to your shock and dismay that you are back where you started.

The hidden resistance is like an elastic band that is anchored in the past. Working against its tensile strength, you stretch toward your goal and feel that you are making progress. When you finally relax or grow tired of this exertion, it pulls you back. This is similar to the experience you had as a child, when you followed your teacher's instructions to sit up straight. You were able to do it temporarily, but then your muscles got tired and you reverted to your regular posture.

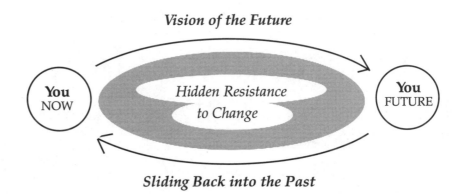

Vision of the Future

You NOW

Hidden Resistance to Change

You FUTURE

Sliding Back into the Past

Figure 2–1.

What is this anchor that ties you to your past and creates a field of resistance that sabotages your efforts?

IDEAS FOR ACTION

Without a solid, conceptual foundation, it is difficult to design the appropriate actions. The following four ideas illuminate why enduring change is so challenging to achieve. We first identify and then briefly explain each idea.

1. All learning is whole body learning.

2. Your nervous system develops action habits that function like a bureaucracy.

3. Habits defend themselves against change.

4. There are two levels of action: internal and external.

1. Whole Body Learning

All learning is whole body learning. It involves your muscles as well as your brain. The thinking, feeling, and kinesthetic dimensions of human life are fundamentally interconnected. How you think influences how you feel. Your moods and beliefs influence your health. Your posture influences your outlook.

No part of you exists outside of the whole of you. Everything you do, you do with your body. You move through space with your body. You touch with your body. You feel with your body. You think with your body. You learn with your whole body. **In everything you do, all of you is involved.**

If you open any medical textbook, you will find entries for the skeletal system, the respiratory system, the circulatory system, the nervous system, the muscular system, the digestive system, and so on. Each is vital in your day-to-day functioning. To understand the wholeness and integrity of physicality, you must study each by itself and in its relationships to every other system. In fact, if you pursue your studies deeply, you find that none of these functions or structures exists outside of the fundamental fact of biological wholeness.

Systems theory looks at the "whole" of the organism and not just at the component parts. It emphasizes the basic principles of internal organization and relationship. When we look at the world in terms of relationships, connections, and integration, we are taking a systems view.

The living human body is not the sum total of these various parts. The whole existed first. All the king's horses and all of his men could not put Humpty Dumpty together again, because they lost the pattern of wholeness that sustained and supported him.

2. The Bureaucracy of Habit

All organizations and systems, including yourself, develop habits through the process of repetition. These habits mediate your relationship with the world. The good news is that habits allow you to pay conscious attention to what is currently important to you, while "they," the habits, are paying attention to all of the details. The bad news is that "they" can distort both your perceptions and your actions. The really bad news is that habits hold on very tightly, as if letting go or changing meant they were dying.

Standing between where you are now and where you would like to be are your habits of perception and action. These habits are written in your nerves and muscles and operate just like a bureaucracy. A bureaucracy is a company's operational infrastructure, the way that things get done.

Every organization, building, community, and nation has a working infrastructure. It is the structure that connects and hold things in their proper place. It is the underlying foundation that supports consistency of action. In organizations and government, the bureaucracy is often perceived to be a deterrent, as much as a help, to getting things done. Bureaucracies prefer to do things in the same way every time. They inherently resist change, especially when it is imposed from the "outside."

Encoded in your muscles and nerves, your "personal bureaucracy" contains your historical patterns of action. The two interconnected sides of the bureaucracy are **what** you habitually do and **how** you habitually do it. Your old patterns can serve as either your ally or your enemy in the process of change.

> *The hardest thing to attend to is that which is closest to ourselves, that which is most constant and familiar. And this closest something is, precisely, ourselves, our own habits and ways of doing things.*
>
> —John Dewey

Each of us has a bureaucracy—**a personal action infrastructure.** Formed by our postures, muscles, and habits of thinking and feeling, it is our way of self-organizing. Our bureaucratic infrastructure allows us to do what we do. Concentrating on rebuilding the infrastructure of personal action is critical if we want to change. Working consciously with our personal action infrastructure opens a doorway to sustainable change. This process of rebuilding unwinds the dominance of our bureaucratic habits.

Our normal ways of thinking, feeling, moving. and sensing are so familiar that we forget they are just habits. Habits can assist or deter our ability to respond to a situation. In our daily activities, we focus on one part of ourselves and become less aware of the rest. Typically, one part stands out more than any other. For example, some people describe themselves more as thinkers than as feelers, and will frequently describe themselves as less aware of their "body" and more aware of their "head." Conversely, people who describe themselves as feelers tend to be more aware of their "bodies" than thinkers.

Because the thoughts, feelings and actions that support our habits are invisible most of the time, we are generally unaware of them. We sometimes notice when a person's habits are unusual or idiosyncratic. Still, most of the time we go about our business with little conscious awareness of our habits. **By expanding our awareness of our own action habits, we accelerate the possibility of changing them.**

However, knowing what new actions you want to take is not enough. Unless the constraints of your personal bureaucracy are addressed, the power of your past will pull you back into your old habits. What was almost in your grasp becomes just a vision of what could have been. The bureaucracy is like a wall that stands between your dreams and a new level of achievement.

3. Natural Defenses

Every organism, whether biological, corporate, or government, has the instinct for self-preservation. Your bureaucracy is no exception. When threatened with change, it reacts immediately. These natural defenses are considered to be the enemy of change. The two responses that follow from this "belief" are to ignore the defenses as if they are of no value and/or to push through them as if they are in the way.

If you accept the premise that bureaucracies are meant to defend themselves, then you can begin to use these resistances as allies in the process of change. Using resistance as an ally is an unfamiliar concept in our culture.

In the martial art of Judo, the student learns how to translate the opponent's resistance into the force that will "throw" them. The same can be true for the force of your habits' natural resistance to change. Reprogramming your habits begins by recognizing and neutralizing the boundary defenses that protect the system from change. From the perspective of your system's habits, the conscious you that wants to change things is an outsider.

It is important to appreciate the personal bureaucracy. Without its assistance, you would have to pay attention to everything you are doing all of the time. By working with it and recognizing its strengths and weaknesses, you can slowly defuse its resistance to change.

If we ignore and depreciate the natural defenses of our own personal bureaucracies, then how can we see what we must do to deal with the resistances in the larger systems in which we are live and work?

4. Two Worlds of Action

The classical disciplines of change, both Eastern and Western, challenge us to perceive and act as a whole being in all of our actions. To do so, we must recognize there are two different types of actions: external and internal. External actions are done in the world. Internal actions are done within ourselves.

External actions are supported by internal actions. Focusing on your goal before you move is an internal action. Getting clear on your motivation is an internal action, as is finding your balance before you move. Before you act and while you are acting, you engage in a coordinated set of internal actions.

Figure 2–2.

These unseen, unfelt, and often unappreciated actions are critical elements in the puzzle of how to change. These actions have popularly been described as the "inner game." The books emphasizing the inner game of tennis, golf, skiing, management, and leadership have argued that the key to success is controlling the negative aspects of our inner game which are our anxiety about the future, our judgments about our past performances, our regrets about what we have failed to do or have not completed, and our self-sabotaging internal imagery and dialogue.

Our every action involves the whole of us, including both our internal and external actions, so we must become increasingly aware of the neglected internal actions. When you express yourself at a meeting or in conversation, your thoughts are colored by your feelings. Your way of gesturing, your pacing, tone, eye contact, and inflection communicate much more than you realize. How you stand or sit or move shapes your presence in the eyes of your audience. These are your habitual internal actions. They produce the person that you know yourself to be and that others recognize. Making small changes in this arena will produce large shifts in your external actions.

The illustration below distinguishes the two kinds of action. Much like an arrow, external actions are released or discharged into the world. Internal actions are more like a circle, a continuous process of self-organization and reflection. The arrows on the circle of internal action represent the different phases or steps that any process must go through.

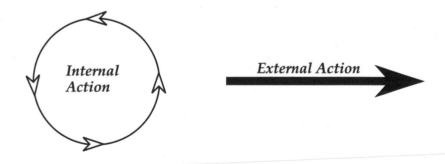

Figure 2–3.

**HOW you pay attention and
WHAT you pay attention to
can change everything.**

3

MASTERING CENTERED PRESENCE

The RETOOLING-ON-THE-RUN strategy does not require you to take time off from work or to go away to a special place in order to learn and change. Your daily activities offer a rich enough playing field. The basic approach is to

- practice wholeness-in-action: *Centered Presence*

- become aware of your habitual actions: *Personal Bureaucracy*

- consciously stretch your repertoire: *Versatility*

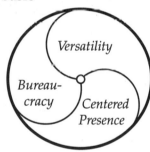

Figure 3–1.

FOUR STRATEGIC KEYS FOR RETOOLING-ON-THE-RUN

Strategy is a necessary step in the translation of ideas into action. It requires asking, *what is the most effective way to use our forces, resources and abilities to accomplish our goals?* The following four strategic keys are essential. They have been taught by teachers in many disciplines.

Our goal is to retool our automaticity, our tendency to act mechanically in situations that we assess to be familiar. Automaticity is a way of handling the anxiety of newness, and is not altogether bad because it allows us to handle the myriad encounters and actions of daily life. However, when it serves to stop us from feeling life as it is *now,* as opposed to how it *was*, then it hinders our capacity to respond with appropriate versatility.

Strategic key #1 **Use every daily activity as the training ground for your learning.**

This involves a shift from the typical model of separating work, home, and study. For example, "I work and then I study," or "I eat and then I study." Each and every daily activity is the appropriate setting for practicing shifts in habits. There is no other place to go to practice and no other time that is necessary. Since everyone is so busy, hardly anyone has the time to go on a study retreat. Those few individuals that are blessed with abundant time often discover that time is not the only critical variable. Knowing what to put your attention on is vital.

> *Everyday life becomes the contest. There must be awareness at every moment: getting up in the morning, working, eating, going to bed. That is the place for the mastery of self.*
>
> —Taisen Deshimaru

If the goal is to change your life, then you have to bring awareness into your everyday actions. This allows you to make course corrections.

Figure 3–2.

The capacity to act with awareness is directly correlated with our sense of presence. When we are present we can respond to that which is **around** us while we maintain attention to that which is in **within** us.

Strategic key #1 handles the ordinary objection of lack of time for learning and study. Using this strategy, practice does not require large blocks of time. It is done while you are doing your work. This makes it more palatable because there is no separation between work and practice. Any of these typical life activities offer opportunities for practicing.

Recreation	Watching television, listening to music, participating in sports, dancing, reading, working out, talking, etc.
Work	Meetings, talking on the phone, interviewing, working on your computer, planning, writing, waiting, speaking at a meeting, etc.
Personal	Eating, shopping, managing children, personal hygiene, making love, dressing, driving, standing in line, etc.

Strategic key #2 **Consciously shift your attention between**
- **what you are doing, *externally*, in the world**

&

- **what you are doing, *internally*, to organize yourself to accomplish that activity.**

Accomplished individuals consistently report that they are aware of both the internal and external levels of action. Your external activities are your normal, everyday actions. Your internal actions stand behind and support your actions in the world. They include your inner dialogue or thinking, mood, posture, gestures, and the mechanics of your movements.

Pay attention to both your work in the world and yourself. When you focus your attention briefly on your internal actions, it acts like a magnetic touchstone to keep your aware of how you act.

This is not done at the expense of the actions that you do but in the service of accomplishment. Every activity can be an opportunity for both accomplishment and learning. Normal life maintenance activities such as shopping, standing in line, or combing your hair can be revisioned as opportunities for learning.

Consciously shifting your attention back and forth between your external and internal actions enhances both your awareness of what is going on and your ability to respond. People notice that something positive and powerful has been added to your presence.

Strategic key #2 is *not* the same as splitting your attention. Rather it is a gentle and brief shift or oscillation. When you split your attention by focusing on two different content areas at once—thinking about home while in a discussion at work—the result is a net loss of effectiveness.

Strategic key #3 **Consciously increase your awareness of the habitual internal actions you make during the course of your daily activities.**

That which you are unaware of, you can do nothing about. Therefore, it is important to expand your bandwidth of awareness to include the subtle, often unrecognized, and undervalued dimensions of experience that strongly affect your behavior and your life. These are different for each person.

By increasing your awareness of these dimensions, you enhance your power to change. Here are some internal action examples using a model of the five components of the personal infrastructure.

Thinking   Includes the activities of inner dialogue (self-talk), self-criticism, judgments of others, affirmations, visualization, imagination, etc.

Feeling   Includes the experiences of detachment, involvement, suffering, passion, avoidance, holding back, repression, suppression, etc.

Movement   Includes noticing and influencing the quality of your movements, its form, flow, coordination and mechanics, relaxing, tensing, etc.

Posture   Includes working with your spine (straightening up, softening, bending, arching); the relationship between your head, shoulders, and pelvis; the overall shape of your limbs and your patterns of tension; etc.

Attention   Includes noticing, directing, and concentrating your awareness; shifting perspectives (figure/ground, big picture/little picture, people/task, self/other); opening yourself for intuition. Attention is the "neutral gear" that opens the door to each of the components.

Figure 3–3.

All of these components are connected, contrary to common belief. What happens to one impacts all of the others. When we think of them as separate, the process of change is slowed. Conversely, working with them as connected, speeds up the process.

Lasting changes begin with small and seemingly subtle actions. Often we can effect change by working with the body tension component of the infrastructure that coincides with the identified "problem." Here are some brief examples of how muscular tension can be tied to both the problem and its solution.

  • A public speaker noticed that he tightened his throat and neck each time he began to speak. He also had a history of losing his voice.

- A district manager noticed that when she sat in a meeting with her boss she collapsed back into the chair as she listened and spoke. She also had a history of being assessed as weak.

- A CEO noticed that every time he gave a speech he got a backache. He realized that he was arching his back in the name of standing up straight.

- A marketing director who had a reputation for aggression and anger noticed that she habitually tightened her guts in her interactions with employees.

- A chief financial officer, assessed by teammates as being difficult to relate to, noticed that he never looked directly at people.

Strategic key #4   **Learn to cultivate Centered Presence as a touchstone in the midst of action.**

A "center" is a focal point from which we perceive, organize, and act. The concept of center is not new. It is found in many disciplines, from architecture to sports, from psychology to the martial arts, and especially in the spiritual traditions. Depending upon the discipline, center has been located in the physical, psychological, or metaphysical realms. Physically, it has been identified by some traditions to be in the lower belly, by others to be in the heart, and by still others to be located in the head.

The whole body is the center is the perspective from which we are working. From this point of view, not just movement, but thinking, feeling, and attention are all actions of the whole body. **Therefore, you should bring conscious awareness of your whole body to all your actions.**

Centered Presence is a powerful exercise that helps you cultivate the experience that your whole body is the center from which you act. It generates an expanded "perceptual space." In this space you literally feel aware of more of yourself. The practice magnifies your kinesthetic sense which alters the width, depth, and focus of your body-attention. There are complementary shifts in the psychological realm as well. Events, stories, and behaviors that have typically triggered an upset no longer evoke the same reaction.

By activating Centered Presence, you can attend to both your activities in the world and your internal state without having to invest additional time. As we bring more of ourselves into our actions, the quality of our results grows.

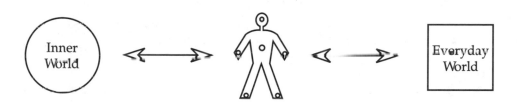

Figure 3–4.

THE PRACTICE OF CENTERED PRESENCE

Centered Presence is much easier to experience than to talk about. Therefore, the next step is to create this experience for yourself. The basic concept behind Centered Presence is to **expand the field of your attention to include your entire body.** Most people have developed kinesthetic habits that leave out or over-emphasize certain parts of the body. For example, some of us are less aware of our feet and might feel ungrounded. Some people are less aware of their hands and therefore feel less connected to others. To assist you in cultivating the practical experience of the whole body as the center, we have identified four key anchor points for your kinesthetic awareness. The dynamic combination of these four points will produce, with sustained practice, an unshakable sense of wholeness-in-action.

Exercise: **Practicing Centered Presence**

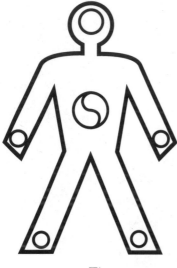

Figure 3–5.

- *Find your feet.*

  Feel your feet touching the floor.

  Notice the pressure and the contact between your feet and the floor.

  Feel the insides of your feet. Feel the muscles and bones.

  Let the sensations grow in strength and spread throughout your body.

  While maintaining this quality of sensation, let a new breath emerge.

- *Find your hands.*

  Feel what you are presently holding or touching.

  Notice the pressure and the contact between it and your hands.

  Feel the insides of your hands. Feel the muscles and bones.

  Let the sensations grow in strength and spread throughout your body.

  While maintaining this quality of sensation, let a new breath emerge.

- *Find your head.*

  Look and listen to what is going on around you and within you.

  Tune in to your senses of smell and taste.

  Notice how your head balances on the top of the spine.

  Let the sensations grow in strength and spread throughout your body.

  While maintaining this quality of sensation, let a new breath emerge.

• *Find your breath.*

Inhale and exhale on purpose.

Focus your attention on the middle of your torso.

Relax and let your breath move to its own rhythm.

Let the sensations grow in strength and
spread throughout your body.

UNITY OF THE BODY AND THE MIND

The power of retooling-on-the-run derives from the paradigm of whole body action. To achieve our goals, it is best to view the body and the mind as a single unit—a bodymind. In both the ancient traditions and modern science, it is taught that the "body" is larger than we had believed. Everything you do, you do with your body. You think with your body. You feel with your body. You respond with your body. Your habits are written in your body.

For the past two centuries, the majority of Western scientists and philosophers have considered the mind and the body as separate entities. In fact, the mind was considered dominant or superior to the body. We were taught that the mind directs the body.

We are in the midst of a global health revolution. The emerging medical discipline of psycho-neuroimmunology asserts that our consciousness affects our physical selves. How we see, believe, and think about ourselves and the world around us has a profound influence upon our state of health and well-being.

This idea of bodymind, which is considered a breakthrough in Western medicine, has long been taken for granted among Eastern cultures. Dr. Deepak Chopra, in his book *Quantum Healing*, contends, "It's not that there's a mind-body connection, mind and body are inseparably one, in every aspect of our physiology, at the level of the cells."

All human actions involve both body and mind. The body without the mind could not successfully direct its action. The mind without the body could not put its intention into action. All of our activities involve acting as a whole. Once we accept bodymind unity, our ways of thinking about our actions start to change. Bringing a sense of wholeness rather than fragmentation to our understanding of being human enhances our power.

It is easy to intellectually appreciate that the body and mind are one unit; it is much more difficult to live that insight.

POWER AND PRESENCE

Presence is vital to power. People respond to your presence even more than they do to your message. People can tell where you are "coming from." They can see where you are seeing from. The way in which you perform your actions reveals your habits of thinking, feeling, and moving. In fact, people see both *what* you do and *how* you do it. They may not be consciously aware of these things, but they do shape the flow and results of your communications. If you want people to respond to you in the way that you want, then the issue of presence is crucial.

In any communication there is an interplay between two factors: 1. what you are saying and/or hearing, and 2. where you are speaking and/or listening from. Researchers agree that between 70 and 90 percent of all communication is **non-verbal.**[1] This includes tone of voice, posture, gesture, and movement dynamics.

What is presence? There are several ways of thinking of presence. It can be physical, mental, emotional or kinesthetic. The most obvious, of course, is the idea of being physically there. However, in the context of retooling it means more than just physically showing up.

Mental presence connotes the ability to think clearly about and to track important components of a situation. People can appear to be present (that is, their body is on the seat) while their attention is far away (mentally absent). No doubt you have had the experience of talking to someone who is not fully "there." It's frustrating to attempt to have an important conversation with someone whose attention has wandered. One common experience for those who lead meetings is to notice that some of the attendees are doing two things at once and are partially present. For example, they may be opening their mail or reading memos while listening to the discussion. We call this behavior *negative double-tracking*.

Being present with *all* of yourself is fundamental to effective action. The kinesthetic component of presence is the experience of your body being awake, aware, and alive. You can feel the energy in your hands, your arms, and your legs, and you can feel the connection between and coordination among them. **When you lose active awareness of any part of yourself, you sacrifice presence and diminish your capacity for action.**

Most people tend *not* to notice when they have lost the awareness of the whole of themselves. What happens when you lose presence? Losing presence is like not being here 100 percent. It frequently feels like your mind is distracted or your attention is split. Some people describe it as feeling "spaced" or "not in their body" or "floating." Others notice their energy is low or that they are slow to respond. Some report not being able to follow discussions or conversations. Your associates may quickly notice that you seem preoccupied or less dynamic. When you lose presence you lose your capacity to access the highest levels of power and responsiveness. Presence and power are fundamentally connected. Your power to act in the world is supported by your inner presence.

Loss of presence begins when your attention drifts. Subjectively, this is like losing a part of yourself. The loss of that part results in the reduction or distortion of your perceptual reality, and you cannot get a "true" reading of the situation. When attention drifts, it produces perceptual blind spots. Data that would normally be available is not. Opportunities that lie in those "missing areas" cannot be acted upon.

Consciously employing a strategy to unify your whole self is vital to effective use of power. The simplest way to create an experience of our whole self being "here" is to use Centered Presence in daily actions.

Not being present can be hazardous to your health. A dramatic example of the potential consequences of not being present comes from a study in the early 1980s of Rahway, New Jersey prisoners who were asked to watch videotapes of individuals walking down a street and identify which of them would be the most likely targets for attack. The prisoners consistently identified those people who appeared to be disconnected in their movements, unclear in their focus and gestures, and acting without mindfulness. People who displayed the carriage of presence and attentiveness were not considered to be good targets.

RETURNING TO CENTERED PRESENCE

Intriguing studies about perceptual-motor coordination were done in the field of developmental optometry several decades ago.[2] This research was prompted by the question, which is better, to maintain your focus for the longest possible time or to be able to return to focus in the shortest time?

The conclusion was that **the length of time that you can stay focused is not as important as how quickly you recognize that you lost it and how quickly you regain it.** We call this the *recovery principle.* It is a systems' concept that applies not only to perceptual-motor coordination, but to the larger issue of presence.

It does not matter how often your attention wanders nor how easily you lose your sense of being centered and present. What does matter is recovering Centered Presence, and remaining there for as long as you do. When you lose it, which you cannot avoid, return to it again. Your task is to recognize the signs of loss of presence as soon as possible. The quicker you can tell, the quicker you can recover and move ahead. The continued use of Centered Presence will dramatically shorten your cycle of recovery.

When you realize that you have lost your Centered Presence:

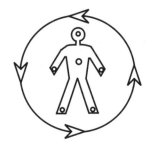

Find your feet.
Find your hands.
Find your head.
Find your breath.

Figure 3–6.

That your attention wanders is not a problem, but a fantastic opportunity to learn about yourself and the world. It is not uncommon to wake up in the midst of what's going on and realize that you are not present. What you do at this moment shapes what happens next. If you do nothing, it is likely that you will continue to be driven by habit. If you remember to return to Centered Presence, you now have the opportunity to discover a new response.

**You are the only person who can reorganize
and reprogram your habits.**

As you cultivate the internal habit of holding your whole body in the field of attention, you return to what is going on more and more rapidly. Like the beat of your heart and the cycle of your breath, attention is a dynamic process. It not only oscillates between being a single-pointed focus and a wide-angle view, it also moves from one point of view to another. This is sometimes called the monkey mind; it has to be tamed but not too tightly controlled.

Each time you pause in the midst of your normal flow and activate Centered Presence, something different will probably catch your attention. With practice, you will wake up in the midst of a habit that you no longer want. You will see and feel what you are actually doing as well as how to shift it.

THE DANGER OF LOSING CENTER

The busier your life is, the more activities you have to juggle. As the pressures build it is not uncommon to find yourself unable to give each issue the energy and attention it deserves. Your attention has to move so fast that it begins to split and fragment. You begin to lose your sense of connection between what you are doing, why you are doing it, and your sense of your own self. To an outside observer, it is clear that you are no longer fully present and centered. Each part of your world gets a little of your attention, depending on how loud it screams or how close to deadline it is. When you are in this state, change is much less important than sheer survival.

Centered Presence can offer a different action alternative to this typical frustrating scenario. It can serve as the switchboard or crossroads between actions, a momentary stopping point where you can refocus on how to move forward into

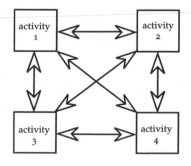

Figure 3–7.

action. Using it, you can shift from one action to another without losing your center.

With Centered Presence, you can pause in the midst of your daily activities and pay attention to the internal coordination of all of your parts. This brings to the foreground your proprioceptive (or muscle) sense, through which you know where each of your body parts is in relation to the others. You can monitor the flow of information and energy. You can shift modes of perception and action. You can fine-tune your intuition. You can run simulation models of your intended actions. You can alter your posture to alter your presence. You can even decide to shift gears and focus on a different task.

When a situation gets stressful and you find yourself reactive, you can interrupt this pattern with the application of Centered Presence. Over time this can become a new habit, freeing up your creative energies and releasing your power to make things happen.

We once observed a nurse who demonstrated this principle in action. In the midst of a disaster, she moved surely and calmly between individuals, offering assistance and completing essential tasks without ever losing her focus or her presence. Despite all the emotional pressure to react to the personal traumas that were going on around her, we observed her strong connection to her core self and her ability to solve problems and serve others.

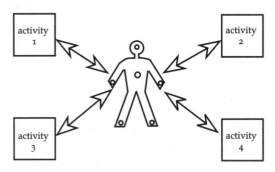

Figure 3–8.

As your own internal coordination grows clearer and smoother, it becomes more responsive to shifting circumstances. Your power to apply these methods magnifies as you consciously develop the habit of shifting back and forth between your internal and external actions.

PLAYING WITH THE RETOOLING EXERCISES

In your encounters with everyday life it is very easy to lose your sense of wholeness. Therefore, the most important action you can take is to recapture it. Each of these exercises is designed to shine a light through the black box of your habits to allow you to see "what you do" so that you can change them. The essence of every exercise is the reawakening of your capacity for wholeness-in-action.

Take the time necessary to go through the exercises. Don't rush through it. Slower is better. As Lily Tomlin once observed, "for fast acting relief, try slowing down." These experiments offer many levels of insight, some of which are gained quickly and others after reflection. They progressively deepen your ability to make changes.

Discovery and exploration are fun. Telling yourself that you "have to" or that you "should" does not make sense. Experimenting with your body and your perceptions can awaken your sense of adventure and open you to a world of exploration. It gives you the opportunity to judge for yourself what is true. Exercises can be done anywhere and the length of time you take to do them can vary. Try them in different settings. Don't get too attached to one time, place, or style. Feel free to modify the exercises to fit your situation.

Accomplishment comes from investment. Learning is possible through repetition. Once is good, and twice much better. The more you put into it, the more you get out of it. Try the exercises a few times. Gently "correct" yourself if you feel you haven't performed as you wanted to. A record of your insights may be helpful for long-term tracking and pattern detection.

Errors are opportunities to clarify how your system works and what to do to be more effective. Do not expect yourself to be perfect. When we begin to practice, we are afraid of making mistakes. Expect to "fail," grandly if possible, for built into failed experiments are the seeds of your next success. If you don't fail once in a while, it's probably an indication that you're not taking risks. The explorations are not intended to be physically or psychically stressful in any way. Since much of what is learned is awareness of how you act, it is important that you feel safe and open to trial and error. No equipment is needed beyond your awareness. Awareness may unfold on a variety of levels, including intellectual, emotional, kinesthetic, visual, or mechanical.

INITIAL EXERCISES

Centered Presence is more than just an interesting idea. Using it, you can make some immediate shifts in your experience and actions. For instance, some emotions have tremendous power over us, leaving us frustrated and feeling out of control. When we are overwhelmed this way, we feel powerless to affect the situation we find ourselves in. Here is a simple exercise that reveals the power for change that practicing Centered Presence offers. In this exercise you observe the impact of Centered Presence upon "negative" emotions. Let your mind be open to noticing the differences in your body.

Exercise: **Centered Presence for resisting the power of negative emotions**

- Sit upright, with your feet planted firmly on the ground, your back erect, your head held up and your eyes gazing straight ahead.

- Place your hands on knees, with palms facing upward, and your fingers stretched open.

- Take several full breaths into the middle of your torso. **Centered Presence = Feet + Hands + Head + Breath**

- Use your imagination to recall a situation in which you were angry.

- Let the memories and the feelings grow in strength.

- While doing this, continue to sit up with your hands and fingers open, your feet on the ground, your spine erect, and your midsection filled with breath.

- Do not tighten your muscles or strain against your posture.

**When your whole body is present in your attention,
negative emotions do not have as much power over you.**

In this next exercise, see what happens when you let your attention get drawn into the negative emotion.

Exercise: Without Centered Presence, Negative Emotions Grow

- Collapse your spine.

- Bend your fingers.

- Sit back and take the weight off of your feet.

- Forget about breathing.

- Now again imagine a situation in which you felt angry.

- Let the memories and the feelings grow in strength.

**Without the support of your whole body, negative emotions gain
the power to tighten and control your perceptions and actions.**

Now let's use this internal act of attention to recover from the negative state and to recapture your innate presence and self-esteem.

Exercise: Changing your experience through Centered Presence

- Return to Centered Presence by sitting upright,
  with your feet planted firmly on the ground,
  your back erect, your head held up, and
  your eyes gazing straight ahead.

- Place your hands on knees, with palms facing upward, and
  your fingers stretched open.

- Take several full breaths into the middle of your torso.
  Centered Presence = Feet + Hands + Head + Breath

The practice of Centered Presence can be used with any negative emotional state. Here are some suggestions.

- I am depressed.
- I am anxious.
- I am afraid.
- I don't deserve it.
- I can't do it.
- I don't want to it.
- I'm confused.
- I'm frustrated.

Practicing Centered Presence makes an immediate difference in your life. It only takes a moment of conscious attention. This initial version of the practice asked you to sit upright. As your experience grows, you can apply it in other postures.

Stretch your experience into life activities. Choose an area in which you'd like to practice (for example, eating, standing in line, walking, showering, driving) and design a preliminary practice regimen. Remember, it is useful to practice a little *all* of the time, but it is impractical to overwhelm yourself with too much practice.

The purpose of waking up in the midst of your daily activities is to create a condition that fosters versatility and presence.

Exercise: Using Centered Presence in Daily Life

The ability to consistently demonstrate versatility in your actions begins with the practice of Centered Presence. To get the greatest value from this practice, use the following steps:

- **remember** to include your whole body in your awareness as you engage in your daily activities;
- **pause** for an instant, in the midst of the goings-on, to let the instructions—*find your feet, hands, head and breath*—activate your muscles and affect your breathing;

- **relax** the muscles that are maintaining your focus (For example, if you are driving ahead with your will, look for excess tension in your face and forehead. If you realize that you are in a reactive mood, then try softening the muscles of your abdomen.);

- **say** the instructions again and encourage your muscles to respond to the words. Notice the small shifts as muscle-tension moves down to your feet, out to your hands and up to your head;

- **return** to whatever you are doing.

Over time, it becomes obvious that when you use this simple exercise, you do feel and act more present and centered. It is as though by repeating the words—*find your feet, hands, head and breath*—you are drawing the outlines of your body in a coloring book. Each time you activate this attitude, you darken the lines, add more details, and fill in more of the colors. As you progress in your practice, a whole new network of neuromuscular connections begins to grow.

If there is nothing else that you get out of this book, let it be this exercise of body-attention. Only time and your own personal practice can prove our premise that the type of learning that produces authentic and lasting change includes *the body.*

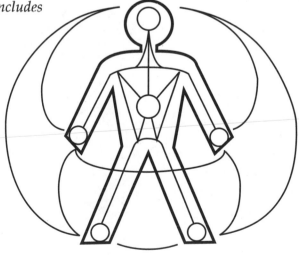

Figure 3–9.

4

TRAINING FOR VERSATILITY

Do not just read, memorize, or imitate, but so that you realize the principle from within your own heart, study hard to absorb these things into your body.

—Miyamoto Musashi, *A Book of Five Rings*

THE MOST DIFFICULT part of writing this book was developing a strategy and a method for translating sophisticated movement exercises into clear instructions, diagrams, and user-friendly commentaries. Although real time retooling, or purposeful change, is not a linear, step by step process, a book, by necessity, must be.

The five infrastructure components—attention, feelings, thoughts, movements, and posture—are equally important and are always influencing each other. However, for the purposes of high level attainment, attention is primary. Attention to your goals, to the details, to your motivation, and to the situation are all factors in achieving success.

The common factor in all of the exercises is body-attention. This cluster of senses—kinesthetic, proprioceptive, and haptic (touch)—is the tangible component of awareness. These senses work close-in; not far-out like the senses of vision and hearing. The actions and responses that take place in this *thicker* realm of experience help to build the concrete foundation of the personal infrastructure. Unless these structures of muscle and nerve impulse are retooled, your dreams of change will remain unfulfilled.

The mind's hand shapes what the mind's eye envisions.

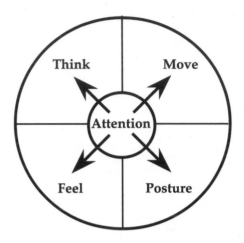

Figure 4–1.

Our uniqueness is found in the way we combine these components to build our personal way of moving through life. Every style or way of being contains elements of all of the components. Your ability to be versatile grows as you increasingly access different ways of perceiving and acting.

THE FOUR EXERCISE SECTIONS

The next four sections of *Retooling on the Run* are for the adventurer who wants to seek out further horizons of possibility. The exercises in each section are designed to fill in, from a different angle, the outline of Centered Presence that you drew with your body-attention. They each emphasize a different component of the personal infrastructure.

The eleven chapters that follow contain approximately sixty exercises together with user-friendly guidelines and commentaries. They are the fruit of cross-cultural and interdisciplinary research that explored what exercises were primary and how they should be presented.

To aid your digestion of this unfamiliar material, retooling stories were developed that captured the dilemmas faced by individuals applying these methods. Drawing upon our consulting and clinical experience, four composite individuals were created, each of a different style and with different desires for change. Each person has four private sessions, one for each section. These stories help you to connect the exercises with real life issues.

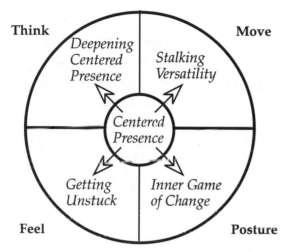

Figure 4–2.

There are two ways to travel through the book. Since all the exercises support the deepening of Centered Presence, you can either work sequentially or you can follow your interests and hunches. In other words, if you are more interested in learning new ways for handling difficult feelings, you might begin with *Getting Unstuck from Your Habits of Feeling.* The next few pages describe what is covered in each of the sections. Moving sequentially allows for a systemic development. Moving creatively allows you to carve your personal path.

At the end of the book, we have compiled a summary of the eleven most essential retooling exercises. We have also included guidelines for personally tailoring your practice to your needs.

Section II: *Deepening Centered Presence*

Centered Presence is an exercise of attention. With practice, you will discover that with a small shift of attention you can subtly reorganize your body so that it becomes easier to access your inherent abilities to be

- grounded, solid, and stable

- connected, sensitive, and flexible

- alert, balanced, and coordinated

- spontaneous, controlled, and flowing

This section is divided into five chapters, each focusing on cultivating another component of body-attention. In *Perceiving with All of You* we begin with exercises that reawaken the connections between intention, breath, and movement. This internal coordination is necessary if you are to make a change that impacts your personal organization.

Building upon this foundation we designed a set of exercises to align your presence with your words (especially **yes** and **no**) and to strengthen the connection between your beliefs and your muscles. When you can feel the tension that accompanies your *negative* thoughts, you can begin to release it. This softens the emotional glue that binds you to the neuromuscular pattern.

In *Working with the Three Centers of Perception* you learn a more detailed set of instructions to deepen your experience of each of the different perspectives and to increase your skill at shifting your attention on purpose.

Following perception comes action. The exercises in *Acting with Your Whole Body* stretch the horizons of your understanding of coordination and control. This chapter contains guidelines for applying these new skills in everyday life.

The exercises in *Knowing with Your Whole Body* help you to listen to the wisdom of your body so you can move forward without unconsciously sabotaging yourself.

In *Practicing for Success* we present a strategy for implementing your personal training. Working with this step-by-step method, you can maximize learning retention and minimize learning decay.

Section III: *The Inner Game of Change*

Centered Presence is an exercise in staying present in the midst of change. It cultivates the strength to wrestle with the conflicting demands of the reorganization process. Every moment pushes you to decide what to **let go of,** what to **add on,** and what to **keep.**

This section has two chapters. *A User-friendly Guide to Letting Go* paints a picture of tension and its release that is very different from the way we were taught. Instead of the idea that letting go means letting go of everything, we present the possibility that it means letting go of only what you no longer need.

The exercises in *Relaxation in Action* propel you to a new skill level in the art of letting go. Instead of focusing on becoming totally relaxed, you learn how to insert moments of micro-relaxation into your every-day, ordinary activities.

The final exercises in this section are devoted to challenging the common thinking that the act of intention is solely a mental act. Instead, you will explore it as an action of the whole body. Many of the obstacles that you encounter and the intense pressures you experience as you push forward toward your goals are the direct result of how you use the tension of intention. You learn how to recognize, relax and rechannel this tension.

Section IV: *Getting Unstuck from Your Habits of Feeling*

Centered Presence is an exercise in participatory observation. With practice, you can develop the ability to stay open to your feelings while also dispassionately observing what is going on. In this body-attitude, it is much easier to release the past and step cleanly into the future.

Turning Your Negative Feelings into Gold is an exploration of a new way of interpreting and working with feelings. As you become aware of the muscle-signature of different feeling states, you can move out of unwanted emotions or evoke desired ones by the process of relaxing tensions and shifting posture.

In *Consciously Changing the Rollercoaster of Feelings* you will learn to use Centered Presence to retool the cycle of your moods. The first step is to identify your personal feeling cycle. The next set of exercises is designed to soften the rigidity of bureaucratic habit. The last exercise teaches you steps for releasing the tensions that sustain your negative feelings.

Section V: *Stalking Versatility*

Centered Presence is an exercise that cultivates the dynamic tension necessary for spontaneous, creative responses. With practice you can develop the strength to maintain this neutral stance while you choose

- to move into an encounter
- to be moved by it
- to move away from it
- to hold your ground

The two chapters in this section are designed to stretch your repertoire of natural responses and give you more choice in how you meet the world.

In the early 1970s, acupuncture was first introduced to the American public. Twenty years later, thanks to the Bill Moyers' television special, *Healing and the Mind*, **T'ai Chi** and **Qi Gong,** the Chinese approaches to exercise, are slowly being recognized as valuable. The material in this section was developed by extracting the best of Chinese exercise and reshaping it to fit modern needs. The exercises are classical in principle yet current in method.

Practicing Intentional Versatility teaches you the fundamentals of a language of movement that fosters the development of versatility. This parallels the way of speaking about strategy and accomplishment that is found in the Japanese classic, *A Book of Five Rings* by Miyamoto Musashi.

In *Retooling Your Personal Strategy* you learn how to use simple movements and postural adjustments to generate the Five Rings within yourself. The commentaries and stories that accompany the exercises reveal some of the psychological and behavioral implications of different ways of moving through life.

**By practicing a particular movement, you can develop
the ability to express a particular quality, style or presence.**

WHAT YOU CAN EXPECT FOR YOURSELF

We asked a group of our clients to tell us, in their own words, what they learned using this approach. They include top and mid-level executives and other professionals from a range of industries throughout the United States. We were particularly interested in what they had to say about long-term benefits. In summary, they consistently reported the following:

Action   better results and a new ease in dealing with challenging situations

Communication   greater clarity, expressiveness, and ability to listen

Style   more decisive, open, assertive, inspiring, grounded, and versatile

Personal   greater control of anxiety, fear, and other negative emotions

Power   enhanced personal presence, authenticity, and acting from center

We are confident that, with practice, you will experience similar results.

DEEPENING
CENTERED PRESENCE

To MAKE A lasting change we have to alter our habitual way of perceiving. Perception is the foundation for our actions and judgments. The way we see ourselves and the world determines the information we have to solve problems or make decisions. It allows us to discern whether something is similar or different from what has come before. When we make a judgment that something is significantly different, it tends to trigger the defenses of our bureaucracy.

Our habits of perception limit and shape our potential to respond. To seek our true capacity, we must unwind our historical patterns. To do this, **we must begin to perceive with our whole self.** It is more than just using your eyes or your intellect. The "seeing" to which we are referring includes your muscles as well as your thoughts and feelings. We call this *whole body perception*.

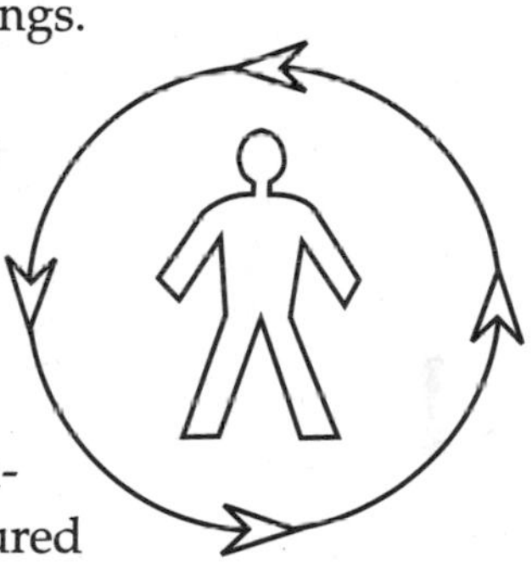

Whole body perception gives us "new eyes." New eyes can give you new data and new data can change everything. It implies an ongoing openness and willingness to perceive the world fresh and to notice previously unrecognized patterns. With new eyes, you can shift your patterns of perception.

This section, "Deepening Centered Presence," will take Centered Presence from being a concept and turn it into a richly textured experience. You will accomplish this in a series of exercises that:

Figure II–1.

1. combine the practice of attention with a simple movement

2. progressively add new realms of awareness and action (for example, breath, intention, thinking, feeling tones, and belief)

3. distill the essence of Centered Presence by exploring the three major perceptual orientations (head, hands, and feet)

4. apply Centered Presence to the issue of problem solving

5

PERCEIVING WITH
ALL OF YOU

To ACHIEVE YOUR goals, your ability to observe must be combined with your capacities for both feeling and doing. Detached observation by itself is not enough. Feeling deeply is not enough. Skill at doing is not enough. By unifying these three realms, lifelong habits can be changed. As you bring more of yourself to everything you do, more power becomes available.

CENTERED PRESENCE IN MOTION

In the world of our internal actions, wholeness rules. Concepts like the body/mind split do not make sense to our organs, our muscles, or our feelings. Yet we have been so well trained in "either/or" logic that we cannot recognize the simple connections between our many parts. In order to shift our internal bureaucracy, we need to use the logic of dynamic wholeness rather than the familiar either/or.

There is no place better to explore this dynamic logic than with the simple action of breathing. Breath has no room for either/or thinking. Can you imagine wondering which is more important, to inhale or to exhale?

Breathing is a dynamic process. It has been going on since the moment of your birth. It is a semivoluntary action. You can control it, but only to a point. You cannot hold your breath forever. At a certain point you will breathe, whether you want to or not. All of the various parts of you are connected to the breath. There isn't any part of you that can live without breath.

Your mood is also reflected in your breath. The breath of happiness is quite different from that of sadness. Your internal conversations, or the stories you tell yourself about how life works and what has happened to you, have a profound influence upon its rhythm and strength. The movements you do in an aerobics class and the meditative flow of a T'ai Chi class produce very different breaths, moods, and conversations.

The process of breathing is not the continuous oscillation between two distinct actions, one called inhale and the other, exhale. Rather, it is one dynamic action that has two phases. As a semivoluntary act, it is found in the interface between external and internal. It can also serve as an ally in your encounters with change.

In the Centered Presence practice, you are asked to find your breath. This simple act draws together and unifies the whole body. It takes the three different parts of you and makes them one. In addition, each of these body parts—feet, hands, and head—is the center of a different mode of seeing, as well as the fulcrum for different ways of doing.

The following series of experiments assists you in expanding and refining your perceptions of action and change. We begin with a simple movement of your hands. The action of opening and closing the hand is analogous to the primordial rhythms of the breath and the heart. By using a very simple movement, your attention can focus on the less obvious phenomena that are going on within you as you do it.

Exercise: Establishing the Rhythm of the Hand

- Sit with feet on the floor, head upright, spine erect, hands on your lap.

- Do the practice of Centered Presence:

Find . . . your feet
. . . your hands
. . . your head
. . . your breath

- Maintaining this stance, open and close your hands.

- Repeat for several moments, rhythmically and attentively.

The object of the first phase of this experiment is to learn the basic form for the movement. For our purposes, the suggested range of motion will be from a closed hand or fist, with your thumb wrapped around the middle joints of the fingers, to a fully extended hand, with fingers straightened and palm stretched.

There are many other ways to do this movement. You could close the hand with the thumb resting on top of the bent index finger. You could place the thumb inside of the fingers. You could move the fingers without moving the thumb at all.

There are also many ways to open your hand. You could leave the fingers still bent, or you could straighten them so far they even bend backward. Notice which way feels normal to you. Then explore doing it in the way described above.

If we asked a large group of people to open and close their hands, you would see a wide variety of methods. Some people emphasize the movement from closed to open, while others would emphasize closing the hand. These differences and all the others that you would be observing are not "body" differences. **They are life differences.** The way you live your life, the ways in which you think, feel, and dream, all shape how you move. The simpler the movement, the more it shows.

Exercise: **Exploring Your Own Rhythm**

- Return to the movement of just opening and closing your hand.

- Do several repetitions of the suggested way.

- Do several repetitions of your normal way.

- Do several more repetitions of the suggested way.

Look for differences in the actual physical movements, in your mood, and in your posture. When you explore the inner workings of your habits, it is imperative that you actively notice the tiniest differences. The more you pay attention to them, the larger they will grow. *In order to make a difference, you have to be able to tell the difference.*

ISN'T THAT INTERESTING?

The process of discovery requires the willingness to notice and wonder. The attitude *isn't that interesting!* is the first step of wondering. This practice can assist you in dealing with your bureaucracy's attempts to stop you from seeing the bigger picture of what is possible.

When you have a big emotional reaction to a situation, it will aid you in observing what is going on without getting overly triggered. *Isn't that interesting?* is a method for opening your curiosity without reactivity. The more you use it, the less identified you become with your actions.

The second use of this mental maneuver is when your first experience of one of the exercises is of "nothing happening." *Isn't that interesting?* now becomes a method for opening your curiosity in the face of boredom. The more you use it, you more you notice.

Using the *isn't that interesting* Method

Stephen, CEO at a computer software company, found himself irritated and frustrated at a request for an increase in salary by his director of operations. He noticed his irritation was producing substantial professional and personal distance between them. His emotional reaction was clouding his normally good executive judgment. As a result, he was only able to see this individual in a negative light. He was unable to have a discussion about the issue without losing his composure.

It was suggested to him that, as an experiment, every time he started to react with irritation and judgment he say to himself, "Isn't that interesting?" He found that the repetition of that statement created in him a state of self-observation that reduced his reactivity. He reassessed his reaction as inappropriate for a CEO, and he then began an effective dialogue with his director.

As this story illustrates, until we can stop and disengage from our reactions, we cannot gain the perspective to see how they can change. When you notice yourself in reaction to an emotional issue or encounter, consider using this procedure. Developing perspective in this way helps increase your capacity for clear, nonreactive response.

HABITS GENERATE PERCEIVED NORMALITY

We perceive and act in the world through the filter of our habits. If we are used to doing things in a particular way, then any other way of doing it feels "wrong." In the F. M. Alexander Technique, an internationally acknowledged method of postural and movement reeducation, there is a teaching story that illustrates this. A woman brings her young child to a session. The teacher works with the child's extremely curved spine and gently evokes a much straighter spine. Standing there, more erect than ever before, the child turns toward his mother and says, "Oh! Mommy, he pulled me *out of shape*."[1]

If your habitual posture is bent over and you straighten up, then your balance sensors will report that you are on the edge of falling over backward. In the same way, when you expand your attention to include your whole body, you do so through your habits of proprioceptive and kinesthetic sensing. These are the senses by which you know where your limbs are and how you are tensing your muscles as you move.

So if, just like the child, you are not used to putting your attention on one part—for example, your feet—then your bureaucracy will tell you that you have found them when you have put only a very small amount of attention energy in that direction. Once you discover that this is the case, then, for a time you will need to feel like you are putting excess attention and energy on that region just to reach the balance point. Over time, of course, this will become a new habit and it will feel like just the right amount of attention.

LINKING THE INTERNAL WITH THE EXTERNAL

In building the communications link between internal and external actions, let's add the breath. We begin by connecting the inhale with the opening of the hands and the exhale with the closing.

Exercise: Coordinating Your Movement with Your Breath

- Begin with one of your hands in the closed position.
- As you inhale, open the hand.
- As you exhale, close the hand.
- Continue for a while.

Three different challenges come together in this one movement

1. coordinating the hand with the breath
2. smoothing the transitions in the breath
3. shifting between having the hand or the breath lead

The first challenge is to coordinate the hand to the breath, so that by the end of the exhale, the hand is closed, and at the peak of the inhale, the hand is fully extended. You will most probably notice that when your attention wanders, these two actions get out of synch. Take some time with this challenge.

The second challenge is to smooth out the transitions in your breath. Explore trying to turn the inhale into an exhale without having to stop and then restart. Instead of just reaching the bottom with your exhale and then climbing back up to inhale, try relaxing as you approach the end of outbreath and letting the inhale happen.

Notice whether you tend to emphasize certain moments in the cycle, for example, the inhale more than the exhale or the bottom of the exhale more than the beginning of it. It is often possible to make quite accurate guesses about the way someone acts in the world from these internal habits.

The third challenge, shifting between having the head or breath lead, is an analogue of the important issue of leading and following. It is essential to the cultivation of flexibility in action. In response to the question, what do I want to change?, two of the most often heard requests are *I want a more commanding presence* and *I want to be a better listener.*

The hand leads the breath.   **The breath leads the hand.**

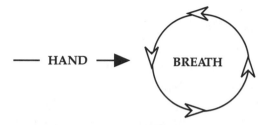 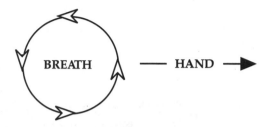

I open my hand and the inhale follows.
I close my hand and the exhale follows.

I inhale and my hand opens.
I exhale and my hand closes.

Figure 5–1.

Anthony

Before he was promoted to vice president, Anthony felt very comfortable and effective using his consensus-oriented style. Even though he was in charge of coordinating his team's activities, he still felt like one of the boys. His strong preference for this horizontal style of working relationship is indicative of a personal infrastructure that is organized around the hands. Anthony's difficulties with taking on a stronger managerial style pointed to an underdevelopment of "feet" (taking a stand) and "head" (deciding what has to be done).

The most difficult obstacle that Anthony has to overcome is his ingrained tendency to base his decisions upon other people's opinions. Cultivating the head aspect of personal organization implies a shift to a more self-directed way of operating. Whenever an individual is asked to fundamentally shift his or her historical style, it is important to reassure them (and their bureaucracy) that they will not lose something precious and vital to their sense of self and self-esteem. Therefore we developed an exercise for him that works with feeling (hands) but from a head (control) perspective.

The mechanics of the exercise were very simple: a rhythmic movement of the hands closing into a fist and then reopening and then closing again. To assist Anthony in cultivating his head strength, we gave him the following instructions: Beginning with his hand in a fist, and before he opened his hand, he said to himself, "I am going to open my hand," and then he opened it. Before he closed it, he said, "I am going to close my hand," and he closed it. This sounds much easier than it really is. Anthony had to fight his old habit's desire to get into the flow of it and "forget" to declare his intent—every time.

After a period of practice Anthony reported that he found himself able to catch himself just before he fell into the old (feeling-based) relationship pattern. This gave him the chance to take a breath and to remember what he wanted to accomplish and what he wanted his team member to do. With this new coordination ability he was able to say, calmly and simply, "This is what I want you do."

THREE MODES OF PERCEPTION

That some people are right-handed and others left-handed is common knowledge and easy to recognize. Just ask someone to pick up a pen and write and their handedness will reveal itself. This is an example of hemispheric dominance. In right-handed people, the left hemisphere of the brain is dominant. The reverse holds true for lefties.

Whether genetic or learned, a pattern of dominance is like a fixed path through the forest. You notice this path before you notice any other. You begin traveling it even before you consciously make a choice. A pattern of dominance relates to the issue of leading and following. In a habit, whether genetic or learned, the roles are fixed and unquestioned.

We are exploring how to change our habits. We want to unfix our patterns of dominance and question our beliefs and interpretations. The exercise of hand and breath that we just explored was designed to begin to loosen the glue of habit. The experiment was to switch between the hands leading the breath and the breath leading the hands. **The goal was to cultivate flexibility in the pattern of dominance.**

In other words, the hands and the breath took turns leading. This is the hallmark of a healthy and flowing hierarchical relationship. When a pattern of dominance becomes fixed, we experience a situation that is often called a patriarchal or hierarchical relationship.

At any given moment, some part of you has to lead. Different tasks often require different leaders. Is there one part of you that leads or tries to lead regardless of the situation?

Another way of examining the issue of pattern dominance is through the model of the three major modes of perception—visual, auditory, and kinesthetic. In every individual one of these modes tends to dominant or lead. Therefore, people can be categorized as being primarily visual, auditory or kinesthetic perceivers. When vision is the dominant mode, what one notices and how one notices is quite different from someone who is either auditorily or kinesthetically oriented. In other words, vision leads and hearing and feeling follow behind, either closely or at a distance. In another person, hearing could be the leader with feeling and vision following.

Almost all current models about how to change are oriented either visually or auditorily. Therefore, to balance the conventional wisdom we wish to emphasize the kinesthetic dimension:

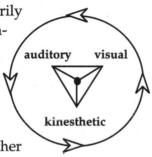

Figure 5–2.

Find your feet.
Find your hands.
Find your head.
Find your breath.

Think with your whole body.
Feel with your whole body.
Act with your whole body.

The kinesthetic sense and the ability to work directly with your neuromuscular system is vitally necessary to make lasting changes in your personal bureaucracy. Just using visual and auditory methods is not enough; we must integrate the kinesthetic dimension into our strong visual and auditory orientations.

WORDS AND MUSCLES

The impact of your words do not just travel outward into the world, they also reverberate through your whole body.

As an example of how words and muscles are connected, let's begin with a simple pair of words: **yes** and **no.** Each one of us uses them differently. Some people are better at yes than at no, and vice versa. Some situations require one more than the other. The series of exercises that follow explore the different movement qualities that yes and no can engender.

Exercise: Finding Yes in Your Body

- Find your whole body.

- Focus on the word **yes.**

- Say it several times, to yourself or out loud.

- Let the sound reverberate through your limbs, torso, and head.

- Let your posture be affected by what the word means to you.

- Return to Centered Presence.

Find . . . your feet
. . . your hands
. . . your head
. . . your breath

The task of reconnecting the verbal and nonverbal dimensions of communication can also be described as reconnecting the head with the rest of the body. Your personal bureaucracy has excellent defenses to stop this from happening.

To assist you in magnifying your whole body awareness, we are going to add something to the practice: varying the intensity of the expression. This will help you to notice which muscles get involved with the **yes** attitude. While doing this exercise, purposefully allow your muscles and posture to shift as you say the word "yes." We know that this is not as easy as it sounds.

Exercise: Intensities of Yes

- Very softly say … yes … yes … yes …
  and let the sound reverberate through you,
  moving your muscles and shifting your posture.

- Speak a little louder … yes … yes … yes …
  and let the sound reverberate through you,
  moving your muscles and shifting your posture.

- Speak even louder … yes … yes … yes …
  and let the sound reverberate through you,
  moving your muscles and shifting your posture.

There are many kinds of *"yes."* Each one moves us differently. There is a yes that is a settling down, a solidifying of one's resolve: "Yes, that is so." It is as though the inner movement traveled from the head's realization down to the abdomen's feeling sense of rightness, back and forth until they merged into a single note or quality of experience.

There is a yes that picks up the back and leads the head to gently rock up and down: "Yes, I see."

There is a yes that begins with an expansion deep within the chest that leads to the throat relaxing and the muscles of the face lifting and softening: "Yes, I feel wonderful."

There is a yes that centers around the eyes and draws together the energy from both head and belly and aims it outward: "Yes, I am ready to do it."

What does YES mean to you?
How does it move you?

Exercise: Intensities of No

- Very softly say … no … no … no …
  and let the sound reverberate through you,
  moving your muscles and shifting your posture.

- Speak a little louder ... no ... no ... no ...
and let the sound reverberate through you,
moving your muscles and shifting your posture.

- Speak even louder ... no ... no ... no ...
and let the sound reverberate through you,
moving your muscles and shifting your posture.

There are many kinds of "no." Each one moves us differently. There is a no that begins with the guts tightening followed by the lips tightening and the face pulling down. As the "No, you won't" grows in strength, the forehead pushes forward to meet the world as if you were a stag preparing to meet a challenger.

There is a no that expresses itself in the almost instantaneous drawing in of the upper belly as though to meet the spine. Your strength and self-esteem appear to have vanished, as the soft vulnerability of your face stands between you and the attacker: "No, please don't come any closer."

There is a no that picks up the spine and lifts the head. With a strong exhale through the nose and a focusing of the gaze, "No, I won't" is your clear, bottom-line answer.

There is the "No, I won't" that purses the lips, stamps the feet, and shines through the eyes.

What does NO mean to you?
How does it move you?

The relationship between yes and no is like the relationship between the inhale and exhale of the breath and the contract and release of the muscles. For some activities we need a long and gentle inhale and a short and strong exhale. For others, a fast inhale with a long, drawn out exhale is what is needed.

Some activities require a strong yes. Others require a soft no. Do you have access to both? What we see is profoundly influenced by what we can do. If there is a phase of the dance between yes and no that you cannot access, then you might not be able to recognize when it is the most appropriate move to make. **What we see affects what we can do, and what we do affects what we can see.**

Figure 5–3.

Exercise: **The Cycle of Yes and No**

- Use the method of the last exercises where you said the word and let the sound reverberate through you, moving your muscles and shifting your posture.

- Say yes and then no with increasing intensity.
  yes . . . yes . . . yes . . . no . . . no . . . no . . .
  yes . . . yes . . . yes . . . no . . . no . . . no . . .

- Do it in reverse.
  no . . . no . . . no . . . yes . . . yes . . . yes . . .
  no . . . no . . . no . . . yes . . . yes . . . yes . . .

- Combine them.
  yes . . . no . . . yes . . . no . . . yes . . . no . . .

- Mix them up.
  yes . . . no . . . yes . . . no . . . yes . . . no . . .

- Invent your own combinations.

- Return to Centered Presence

Find . . . your feet
. . . your hands
. . . your head
. . . your breath

DAMPENING THE DIFFERENCES

Habits of perception defend themselves just like any other habit. Your personal bureaucracy prefers normality. It doesn't want you to notice or feel anything that might awaken you. The exceptional and the unusual are dangerous to the status quo. Therefore, they are pushed aside or ignored.

This can show up as, "When I first did the exercise I noticed some differences, but the more I did it, the easier it became until there was no difference at all any more." The bureaucracy of the nervous system is like a filter in an electronic circuit that dampens out the "extraneous" oscillations to produce a "smooth" output.

It takes a special strength to let your words reverberate through your muscles. True responsiveness is more than just sensitivity. There is a special power that comes with depth of perception. As you grow in your ability to feel what you say, there is a corresponding enhancement of your ability to see yourself clearly and honestly. The natural result is that you can see what is going on around you, make better choices, and act more effectively.

Authentic change is produced by following your vision and walking your talk. Being moved by what you say and see grounds and energizes your purposeful actions. The more you feel what you mean, the less repetitions are required. The more you experience and the faster you allow it to happen, the shorter is your path.

WORD-MUSCLE DISSONANCE

The muscular reverberations of our words radiating outward forms an integral part of our presence as perceived by others. In these last few exercises we have been working to create a harmonious sound-feel. When word and muscle work together we perceive a sense of rightness. However, when they are at odds, they produce a dissonant feeling in the listener.

We often translate this word-muscle dissonance to ourselves as "something is not quite right here." As we listen to ourselves, there are so many internal voices each claiming to have the truth, how can we tell which ones are to be trusted?

The following exercises are to explore the phenomenon of word-muscle dissonance. The exercises are like the compulsory figures in ice skating or the katas (martial dances) in karate. The precision, strength, and awareness that they help cultivate can serve as guideposts as you explore the very complex amalgam of beliefs, reactions, postures, movements, and other learnings that form the neuromuscular bureaucracy of your habits.

Exercise: Word-Muscle Dissonance

- Shape your posture to fit what happened when you said **yes.**

- Say **yes** in this muscular state and notice the coherence or sense of rightness.

- While remaining in this same muscular state, say **no.**

  Notice the internal dissonance this produces.
  *How do your muscles want to shift in response to **no**?*
  What internal dialogue and mood shifts did this produce?

- Shape your posture to fit what happened when you said **no.**

- Say **no** in this muscular state and notice the coherence or sense of rightness.

- While remaining in this same muscular state, say **yes.**

  Notice the internal dissonance this produces.
  *How do your muscles want to shift in response to **yes**?*
  What internal dialogue and mood shifts did this produce?

Exercise: The Muscles of Love and Hate

- Say, **"I love you"** and let your muscles and posture shift to fit this.

- Say, **"I hate you"** and let your muscles and posture shift to fit this.

- Now, shape your posture to fit **love,** and say, **"I hate you."**

  How does the dissonance show up for you
    —in your muscles?
    —in your mood?
    —in your thoughts?

- Now, shape your posture to fit **hate,** and say, **"I love you."**

How does the dissonance show up for you
    —in your muscles?
    —in your mood?
    —in your thoughts?

These exercises will sneak in under the defense screen and begin to loosen the glue that binds you to the past. You can explore this same process with other words or statements. Here are some examples: *"I'm going to work"* versus *"I'm coming home."* Or *"I feel tense"* versus *"I feel relaxed."* You can use any words you wish.

When you do these exercises, first, let the reverberations of the sound spread through your limbs, torso, and head, reshaping your muscles and posture. Second, notice the shifts in your feelings and thoughts. You can also explore the word-muscle connection by first assuming the posture of one word and then saying another, very different one. As you become more and more sensitized, you will begin to notice a whole new dimension to the conversations you are having.

THE MUSCLES OF BELIEF

The power of belief shapes your actions, your experiences, and your results. Believing involves the whole body. Your beliefs are not found only in your thoughts, they are found everywhere, even in the subtle shapes of your posture and in the dynamics of your movements. Your habitual ways of reacting to people, events, and feelings tell the story of your beliefs. If you are to make the changes you desire, you must harness this power of belief.

As you believe, so you behave.
As you behave, so you become.
As you become, so becomes the world.

In itself, belief is not a problem. Like the bureaucracy, it is a necessary factor in the process of accomplishment. It acts like a lens, focusing the power of your imagination, intellect, and vision. It brings together your attention and energy so you move forward into action.

The problem lies in how you **believe** in your beliefs. Do you hold them with too much tension or not enough? How do you defend them and how do they defend themselves? The issue of the accuracy of your beliefs is not the subject of this book. We are concerned with recognizing and neutralizing the bureaucratic defenses that shield your beliefs from clear observation.

The next set of exercises explore the "physical" tension side of belief. The first step is to discern the muscular signature difference between a positive, success-generating belief and a negative, self-sabotaging one. An example of a positive belief is, I am a excellent learner. An example of a negative one is, I am stupid. As your "mental" belief becomes more "physically" tangible to your perceptions, you can work more effectively to unravel its attachment to you so you can release your attachment to it.

Exercise: The Muscles of Positive Believing

- Choose one of your **positive, success-generating beliefs.**

- Say it to yourself several times each time making it more believable.

- Let your muscles change to fit this belief.

  Let your facial expression shift.
  Let your belly muscles shift.
  Let your breathing rhythm shift.
  Let every muscle in your body shift to fit this belief.

- Repeat several times until the feeling grows strong and unmistakable.

- Return to Centered Presence.

Find . . . your feet
   . . . your hands
   . . . your head
   . . . your breath

Exercise: The Muscles of Negative Believing

- Repeat this exercise with one of your **negative self-sabotaging beliefs.**

- Say it to yourself several times each time making it more believable.

- Let your muscles change to fit this belief.

  Let your facial expression shift.
  Let your belly muscles shift.
  Let your breathing rhythm shift.
  Let every muscle in your body shift to fit this belief.

- Repeat several times until the feeling grows strong and unmistakable.

- Return to Centered Presence.

Find . . . your feet
. . . your hands
. . . your head
. . . your breath

UNRAVELLING YOUR BELIEFS

Each belief has a different feel. The difference may be subtle, but that does not make it any less important. Subtle perceptions are the essence of skillful actions. By training yourself to recognize the signs of a negative belief when you find yourself in a no-stress situation, you increase the odds of being able to recognize it when it's important that you do so.

Here are a few guidelines to assist you in delineating the differences. Each time you do the exercise notice a bit more. Just as with statistics, you need multiple repetitions to gather enough observations to uncover a pattern.

Exercise: Noticing the Many Facets of Belief

Choose a belief that you want to explore. It can be either a negative or a positive belief. Use the questions to guide your awareness and increase your observational ability.

- Say the belief to yourself and let your whole body speak back to you.

    Into what posture are your muscles shaping you?
    Is your spine becoming more erect or more collapsed?
    Are you sitting (or standing) more forward or to the back?
    What else do you notice about your posture and body tension?

- Say the belief to yourself and let your whole body speak back to you.

    What is your face telling you about this belief?
    Are you smiling more or less than before?
    What are your eyes doing?
    Are they opening up or are they narrowing?
    Are you looking out at the world or in?
    Are they focusing on a point or are they looking all around?

- Say the belief to yourself and let your whole body speak back to you.

    How are you gesturing?
    How do you move your hands?
    Are you more expressive or less?
    Are you reaching out, pulling back, cutting through,
    or holding on with your gestures?

- Say the belief to yourself and let your whole body speak back to you.

    What internal conversations turn on?
    What is the topic and what is its feeling tone?
    How many voices are taking part?
    Is it a discussion or a guilt trip?
    Is it heading toward the future or is it going back to the past?
    Are you leading the conversation or are you following
    or are you just watching?

Different beliefs shape you differently. The next time you find your-self wondering if you are getting caught up in an old and unwanted belief, scan yourself for the muscular cues that are associated with it. Begin to loosen the hold old beliefs have on you and assert with clarity and confidence the beliefs that fit your values and your goals.

Exercise: Retooling Your Response to a Negative Belief

- Choose a **negative belief** or one that you want to test out, for example, "I can't do it" or "No one respects me."

- Say it to yourself several times, each time making it more believable.

- Let your muscles change to fit this belief.

  Let your facial expression shift.
  Let your belly muscles shift.
  Let your breathing rhythm shift.
  Let every muscle in your body shift to fit this belief.
  Let the internal conversations grow louder.

- Repeat several times until the feeling grows strong and unmistakable.

- Maintain this tangible feeling and *find your feet.*

- Let the muscles that correspond to the belief begin to soften, and let the energy flow into your legs and feet.

- Keep repeating the belief as you *find your hands.*

- Let the muscles that correspond to the belief begin to soften, and let the energy flow into your arms and hands.

- Maintain this tangible feeling and *find your head.*

- Let the muscles that correspond to the belief begin to soften, and let the energy flow into your neck and head.

- Holding the belief together with feet, hands, and head and *find your breath.*

- Stop telling yourself this negative story.

- Breathe and return to Centered Presence.

 **Find . . . your feet**
        . . . your hands
        . . . your head
        . . . your breath

The belief itself is not the problem. The difficulty lies in how it is held. In other words, it is your muscular *belief* in the belief that hinders you. **A "negative" belief that is held gently does not have the same effect as when it is held tightly.**

Exercise: Unwinding the Power of the Belief

- Go back to the negative belief that you used for this exercise.

- Say it to yourself again.

- Does it have the same charge?

- Go through the process several times until the belief has almost no hold upon you.

- Try this with other beliefs.

> **The practice of Centered Presence
> takes the bite out of the negative
> and deepens the positive.**

You do not just have one belief, you have many, and they may not all agree with each other. Each of these beliefs is also built upon other beliefs.

A belief is a particular patterning of muscular tension. This complex web of believing to which we are referring is a complex web of tensions. Letting go in this context is not a simple, "just do it" type of action. Your habits of experience and action are built upon your habits of believing.

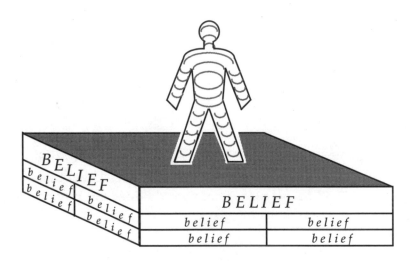

Figure 5–4.

Each time you employ Centered Presence you will find your experience of the practice somewhat different. Every shading of belief requires a different direction of release. There are times when *find your feet* is the key. At other times it might be *find your hands* or *head* or *breath*. It took time for your bureaucracy of belief to build up this tension. It will take time for it to unwind. Each moment you do the best you can and then let it go.

6

WORKING WITH THE THREE CENTERS OF PERCEPTION

PERCEPTION INVOLVES THE whole body. The three major perceptual orientations—head, hands, and feet—each represent a different neuromuscular framework or lens. Through each you see the world quite differently. We will explore what the world looks and feels like from each of these centers of perception.

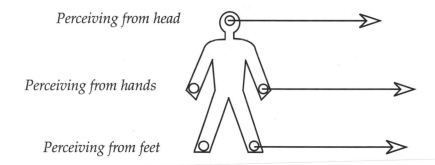

Perceiving from head

Perceiving from hands

Perceiving from feet

Figure 6–1.

Each way of seeing yields different data, sensations, awarenesses, and judgments. We were not shown these differences in our schooling. We assume that everyone is perceiving from the same place, though sometimes with a different range of focus. That is, some watch details and some see big pictures. Social and psychological research has now clearly demonstrated that each of us has significant filters on our perceptions. Some filters are psychological or emotional, some physiological, some are cultural, and some are cognitive or belief based.

Where you perceive from not only gives you a different view of what you are doing but it also changes it. Developing flexibility in shifting from point of view to point of view has two important advantages. First, it loosens up the layers that bind you to your habits. Second, since not every action is meant to be done from the same perspective or center, you can shift to the one that fits the task at hand. Doing your taxes and making love are not done from the same place.

By discovering the subtle and not so subtle differences that each perspective brings to your experience of life, your everyday perceptions are made richer. Your ability to use Centered Presence will grow as you separate and reconnect the components of perception.

The learning process of this section has three sequential steps:

1. **Find.** You will learn a simple method for deepening your experience of each of the perceptual centers.

2. **Move and Speak.** You will have the opportunity to practice connecting your actions to each of the major perceptual orientations.

3. **Know.** You will learn a method for evoking the truths that lie behind your habitual answers.

THE HEAD

The **head** is the perceptual center most concerned with awareness, concentration, focus, thinking, and planning. While everyone has one, we each use it differently. For some, it is their core way of seeing. For others, it is used in support of another perceptual center, for example, when the heart leads and the head follows.

It is possible to have too strong a head orientation. The reverse is also possible. When your head is too strong, it is easy to diminish the importance of your feelings and sensations. When your head orientation is too weak, it is easy to get lost in your feelings, lose focus and have difficulty with decision making.

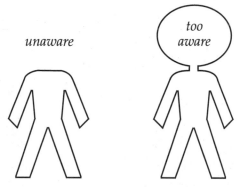

Figure 6–2.

Here are several questions to assist you in noticing where you are on the head center continuum.

> *Do you get so caught up in what you are doing that you forget why you are doing it?*
>
> *Do you get stuck in your feelings and find yourself unable to think clearly?*
>
> *Do you have difficulty making decisions and plans?*
>
> *How important is it to be aware?*
>
> *Is it very important to be in control?*
>
> *Do you have to know where everything is?*
>
> *Is designing a plan more interesting to you than doing the work to make it happen?*
>
> *Is the purpose of your body to carry around your head?*

What perceptual center you need to use depends upon the situation. Where your personal bureaucracy wants you to be is where you have always been. **But what do you want?**

Exercise: **Find Your Head**

- Find your head.
- Use your eyes and look to see where you are.

- Use your ears and listen to what is being said.

- Notice how your head balances on the top of the spine.

- Take a breath and exhale, saying, "Ah ha!"

- Use this new energy to straighten up.

You may have to do this several times for the effect to grow strong enough to be easily observable and able to influence your perception. You will periodically lose your awareness of the head and have to find it again. Then you will lose it again. No problem. This is the natural oscillation of attention, forgetting and remembering.

Christopher

Christopher, a fifty-two year old Silicon Valley executive, had a reputation for being able to handle challenging turnaround situations. With his strong, commanding presence and a tremendous work drive, he was able to push his team to achieve difficult goals and deadlines. However, his personal life and physical health were showing signs of severe stress. His goal for our work together was to become even more effective but with less stress.

Christopher could best be described as being mind or head oriented. With his command center "above the neck," he did not notice other people's responses to him. When he was in his driven state, he did not even notice his own body or feelings.

For his first practice, he was given the Centered Presence exercise. With repetition he learned that feeling was not as big a deal as his "head" had always believed. By asking him to expand his current field of attention to include his entire body instead of asking him to just pay more attention to other people, we were able to neutralize his bureaucracy's natural resistance to change. The Centered Presence exercise communicates the nonverbal message that the head has always been connected to the "body."

The first shift that Christopher reported was that he regained his focus and felt more calm and relaxed. Instead of feeling as if everything was pressing in on him, he felt more space and more time. He discovered that if he used the Centered Presence exercise *(Find your feet ... hands ... head ... breath)* before he focused on a work challenge, he regained his sense of power and flexibility. Feeling his rhythm, he could accelerate without losing connection to either himself or the people and projects with which he was dealing. With his body working together with his mind, he found it much easier to control his personal fears and anxieties as well as show others that he was, in fact, a deeply caring individual.

THE HANDS

The **hands** are the perceptual center most concerned with touching, holding, reaching, feeling, and relating. We each use these faculties differently. For some, this is their prime mode of perceiving. For others, it is used in the support of another perceptual center.

It is possible to have too strong a hands orientation. The reverse is also possible. When your hands are too strong, it is easy to diminish the importance of your thinking and sensing. When your hands orientation is too weak, it is easy to get lost in your thoughts, not feel connected, and find it difficult to relate.

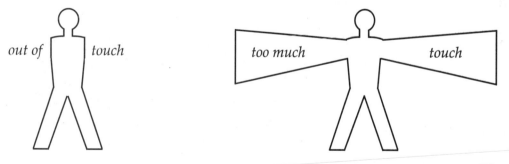

Figure 6–3.

Here are several questions to assist you in noticing where you are on the hands center continuum.

Do you often feel out of touch?

Are you preoccupied with what you think at the expense of what you feel?

Do you feel distant from other people?

Do you feel distant from yourself?

Is it difficult for you to socialize?

Are you too concerned with being in touch?

At a meeting, is it more important to deal with someone's emotional upset or stay with the agenda?

Do you speak from your feelings more than from what you think?

Is it very difficult to end a relationship?

To cultivate a stronger foundation for your touch and relationship perception, you can use this expanded version of "Find your hands."

Exercise: Find Your Hands

- Find your hands.
- Use your tactile senses to feel what you are touching, whether it is an object or your own hand.
- Notice the pressure and the contact between it and your hands.
- Take a breath and exhale, saying, "Ohhh."
- Use this new energy to soften your chest and your groin.

For the effect to grow strong enough to be easily observable, and to therefore be able to influence your perception, you may have to do this several times. Remember, you will periodically lose your awareness of your hands and will have to find them again. Then you will lose them again.

Dorothy

Dorothy was a top executive in a large midwestern corporation. She headed a large professional team using a demanding, hard to please style. She had consciously sacrificed personal relationships and family for her career. She was becoming frustrated with her style and its consequences for her life. Her goal was to become even more powerful while at the same time learning to work with her feelings.

Dorothy had always loved to go head to head with powerful people. She relished the intensity and excitement of making things happen despite the obstacles. Her basic method was to see what she wanted to do (head), take a stand (feet), and then go for it. The down side of this approach was that her hands (feelings) were only used for pushing and grabbing. The missing element in her long-term strategy for success was people skills, in particular allowing others to feel that she cared.

The simplest exercise for cultivating the presence of caring would be to emphasize the hands' component of Centered Presence. However, when dealing with an individual whose personal bureaucracy is programmed to be a fighter, the practice has to be presented from a stronger perspective. To such a person, the experience of "hands" by themselves feels weak, and that to them is intolerable. The training concept shifts to cultivating caring with power.

The first step is to cultivate a body sense of inherent power and stability (feet). This is very different from the head's voice, which states "I am powerful." By removing the "I" from the power, the confrontational tone is automatically diminished. Dorothy was taught to stand tall, with one foot slightly in front of the other. This posture promotes stability and freedom of movement. The second step was for her to *"Find her feet."* This would encourage the fighting energies of the head to settle down and grow calmer.

The next step was to bring her hands into the picture. Using her new body (feet) feeling as a foundation, she was taught to reach forward with her hands just to the level of her navel and turn them slightly palm forwards. Still maintaining the strength in her legs, the next step was to subvocalize the (hand) sound "Ohhh." This sound together with the gesture generated the presence of caring. When combined with the legs, Dorothy was able to present herself as being open and really listening while at the same time she still felt strong. Over time she discovered that this "acting" exercise became real. She found it easier and easier to bring forth her caring qualities without loss of her driving power.

THE FEET

The **feet** are the perceptual center most concerned with balance, stability, and movement. We each use these faculties differently. For some, this is their prime mode of perceiving. For others, it is used in the service of another center.

It is possible to have too strong a feet orientation. The reverse is also possible. When your feet are too strong, it is easy to diminish the importance of your thinking and feeling. When your feet orientation is too weak, it is easy to feel ungrounded, unprotected, and find it difficult to focus on details.

ungrounded

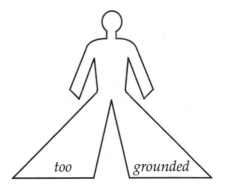

too *grounded*

Figure 6–4.

Here are several questions to assist you in noticing where you are on the feet center continuum.

Do you believe that you are grounded enough?

Are you able to maintain your sense of integrity and dignity without having to fight to prove it?

Do you notice or are you interested in the details of a project?

Are you able to stay calm under pressure?

Are you too concerned with being grounded?

Do you prefer to go one step at a time even when it is time to leap into the unknown?

Are you overconcerned with details?

Do you easily show how you feel or do you keep it well hidden?

One of the easiest tests for ascertaining too much or too little ground-edness begins by standing still. The first measure is: **can you stand still?** The second is: **is it difficult or easy for you to move off of a position?**

To cultivate a stronger foundation for your balance and stability perception, you can use this expanded version of "Find your feet."

Exercise: Find Your Feet

- Find your feet.
- Feel them touching the floor.
- Relax your face and mouth.
- Let your shoulders drop.
- Take a breath and exhale, saying, "Ahhhh."
- Soften your belly.

You may have to do this several times for the effect to grow strong enough to be easily observable. You will periodically lose your awareness of your feet and have to find them again. Then you will lose them again. No problem. This is the natural oscillation of attention.

Pauline

Pauline was the head of sales for a major East Coast firm. She was known for her charismatic personality and "go getter" attitude. She always had more on her plate than seemed humanly possible, juggling multiple projects and an overwhelming travel schedule as she tracked all of her direct reports from around the country. Her goal was to develop a strong ability to handle completions and details to match her well-cultivated ability to dream, create, and think big.

Pauline's personal operating system was oriented around future visions and passionate communication. In the context of the Centered Presence exercise, she emphasized her hands (touch) and head (see).

Her greatest weakness lay in completing or even noticing the details of a project (feet).

Since details live in the here and now, Pauline was taught a version of Centered Presence that emphasized her feet and legs. To help her develop the strength to resist the pull toward the big picture and future possibilities, she was given a practice to do while sitting. The essence of it was to feel her buttocks settle into the chair. This drew her attention "out of the clouds" and back down to earth (the home of details).

As soon as she did this she realized that she passionately avoided feeling heavy or weighted. Her habitual interpretation of this body state was "I feel stuck. I feel passionless. I want to get out of here. I want something exciting." To clarify this point, we had her shift back and forth between finding her head and hands and then finding her feet. Every time the energy went up again, she felt comfortable. Every time the energy went down, she felt uncomfortable, stuck and passionless.

Through this process Pauline saw that when she used comfort as her guide she would, of course, choose to be up and excited, and hence detail-phobic. She realized that in order to make the change that she wanted to make, in other words, to learn to handle details more effectively, she would have to accept and even choose to feel uncomfortable and heavy. After only a few weeks practice Pauline reported that even though it still felt strange to add more "feet" to her life, she was beginning to feel comfortable with and even enjoy handling the details.

BREATHING THE CENTERS TOGETHER

Breathing is a semivoluntary act. Being semivoluntary, breathing connects directly to both your creative and spontaneous self as well as to your bureaucratic self. By paying more attention to your way of breathing, you will be able to notice more quickly when you are in the habit mode versus your creative mode. If you can notice it, you can change it. In each of the practices of perception and presence, you used your breath.

For the **feet,** you exhaled with the sound of "**Ahhh.**"

For the **head,** you used the sound of "**Ah ha!**"

For the **hands,** you used the sound of "**Ohhh.**"

There is nothing magical about this. When you make the sound of "Ahhh," it is followed by a current of downward moving relaxation. The sound of "Ah ha!" produces a lifting upward. "Ohhh" generates a rounding of the spine and a current of relaxation to your limbs.

This next exercise seduces the bureaucratic defenses into relaxing control. It uses the way of breathing that your body uses when you are asleep and the bureaucracy is off-line.

Exercise: **Breathing by Relaxing**

- First, inhale and exhale on purpose.
- After a few breaths, at the end of the next exhale, wait.
- Do not try to breathe but do not hold your breath.
- Send messages of relaxation to your torso and throat.
- Let the breath emerge in its own way, without judging it.
- Let the exhale happen in its own way.
- Let the breath move to its own rhythm.

This practice produces two seemingly contradictory phenomena. On one hand, it is very soothing and peaceful. On the other, it can make very obvious how much tension you ordinarily carry. Just go with the flow. Over time, the tension will gently wash away.

The practice reminds us that **allowing an action to occur is another way to look at control.** Letting go and holding on are not really opposites. It is just that we are so used to holding on with much too much tension, letting go seems like a big deal. To see the world brand new we have to let go of how we have seen it in the past. By practicing with your muscles, you are also training your perceptions.

CULTIVATING PERSPECTIVE

The ability to consider a decision from multiple points of view (including the best value for the whole) is a fundamental practice for leaders to cultivate. While activating Centered Presence, the leader should examine an issue or problem

1. from the perspective of the **whole organization**

2. from the point of view of the **individual** or the **part of the organization**

3. consider the point of view of the **whole system** again before

4. **deciding** and **putting the decision into action.**

Many of the problems we face within organizations can be traced back to a fundamental misunderstanding. Members of companies often forget that they are part of the same organization. They think the other departments are their competitors and enemies. When we forget our fundamental organizational interconnectedness, we can justify counterproductive behaviors against other executive team members as "politically necessary." Our mind-set gets structured and we act as if our business partners are our problems, not our allies.

The way we view the world determines much of what we observe. The challenge is to widen our circle to include our teammates so that we can work together constructively. Just as if we would not do things to injure members of our own family, we must remember that our company's employees are part of our family as well, committed to the same objectives and strategies. The leader must hold and model that perspective for everyone to see and learn from. When you adopt a viewpoint that all members of the organization are important and need to be considered, you can begin to understand that any action you take that counters that perspective is harmful.

The leader's job is to show how respecting the integrity and accountability of every piece of the company is vital. True leaders are role models. We admire and follow them because they apply their deepest insights to complex human situations. Guided by principles and clear values, leaders demonstrate the inner game of leadership, walking their talk in all aspects of life and work.

Try this practice to observe how you can cultivate the multiplicity of perspectives that are essential to excellent decision making.

Exercise: The Corporate Perception Practice

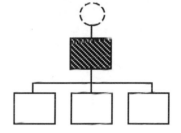

- **Finding the CEO Perspective**
  1. Tune in to the role and responsibilities of the CEO.
  2. Consider your job or task at hand from that point of view.
  3. Notice what would stand out or be emphasized from that perspective.
  4. Let go of the CEO perspective and resume attending to your role.

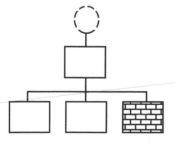

- **Finding the Operations Perspective**
  1. Tune in to the role and responsibilities of Operations.
  2. Consider your job or task at hand from that point of view.
  3. Notice what would stand out or be emphasized from that perspective.
  4. Let go of the Operations perspective and resume attending to your role.

• **Finding the R & D Perspective**
1. Tune in to the role and responsibilities of R& D.
2. Consider your job or task at hand from that point of view.
3. Notice what would stand out or be emphasized from that perspective.
4. Let go of the R & D perspective and resume attending to your role.

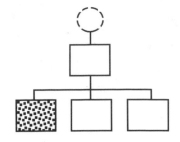

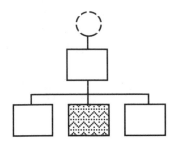

• **Finding the Sales Perspective**
1. Tune in to the role and responsibilities of Sales.
2. Consider your job or task at hand from that point of view.
3. Notice what would stand out or be emphasized from that perspective.
4. Let go of the Sales perspective and resume attending to your role.

• **Finding the Mission Statement**
1. Tune in to the vision and values of the mission statement.
2. Consider your job or task at hand from that point of view.
3. Notice what would stand out or be emphasized from that perspective.
4. Let go of the mission perspective and resume attending to your role.

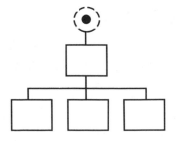

- **Finding the Whole Perspective**
  1. Begin systematically alternating your attention to the role and responsibilities of each perspective.
  2. Notice what would stand out or be emphasized from those perspectives.
  3. Try to hold the whole perspective by attending to each in turn and then all at once.
  4. Let go of the whole perspective and resume attending to your role.

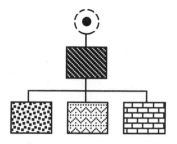

Concentrating on just one of its functions gives a distorted and inaccurate view of the wholeness of a living organization. If we were to look at **any** whole, we would discover the same phenomena. From a systems perspective, the attempt to arrive at a solution to a problem that exists within a whole (organization) without taking into account the relationship of the part to the whole will yield a suboptimal result. In other words, it would not really work. You might make the part better, but at the cost of a decrease in either another part or in the overall functioning of the whole organization.

If any organization is dominated by one part, problems inevitably occur. To be effective, an organization must take into account the multiple needs and positions of its various components. Imagine the consequence if the company does not hear the concerns of its customers regarding distribution issues because it is only concerned with sales, not delivery. Or, for another example, the sales organization that does not pay attention to the finance component of its organization and therefore does not know its situation with collections.

To be our most successful, we must hear, integrate, and consider the component stakeholders within an organization. Just like an individual, an organization must integrate its diverse views if it is going to act from the perspective of the whole.

Every fight is between different angles of vision, illuminating the same truth.

—Mohandas K. Gandhi

When your field of attention is unbalanced in any way, it leads to actions and decisions based upon partial realities. When you are **unaware** of your bias, it is easy to mistakenly believe that you are operating from clarity and wholeness. When you have a balanced field of attention, your actions and decisions emerge from a complete picture or reading of the world.

When we think, feel, and move as a whole, we are more likely to make wise decisions.

7

ACTING WITH YOUR WHOLE BODY

A CENTER OF perception is also a center of action. "Where" you move from has a profound effect upon the quality and appropriateness of your actions. The fighter's punch and the lover's touch do not begin in the same place. The Japanese samurai moves from a very different place than the classical ballet dancer.

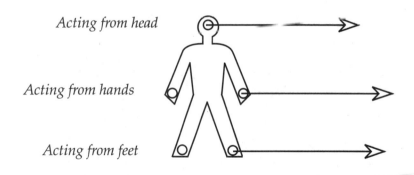

Acting from head

Acting from hands

Acting from feet

Figure 7–1.

The same movement performed from a different center has a very different impact upon oneself and the environment. The way of being that suits a particular situation or goal may not fit another as well. A way of being is also a way of being centered.

From time to time, we face situations that require us to cut through a morass to get to the heart of an issue. To do this, **you need all of your**

centers. You need to bring together the clarity of your head and the calm of your legs with the compassion of your arms.

MOVING FROM THE HEAD

With your eyes and ears, you notice the world-out-there. Having access to the power of the head, you can maintain the "objectivity" to discern what is really going on. By cultivating this perceptual channel, it is easier to focus on what is important and to strategize the best way to achieve your goals.

Exercise: **Moving from the Head**

- **Find your head.**

  Use your eyes and look to see where you are.

  Use your ears and listen to what is being said.

  Notice how your head balances on the top of the spine.

  Take a breath and exhale, saying, "Ah ha!"

  Use this new energy to straighten up.

- Move your hands in the simple rhythm of opening and closing.

- Look at your hands and their movement as though from a distance.

- Explore turning the hands so that you can observe the movement from different angles.

- Study the shape and rhythm of the movements as though you were watching either someone else or a machine.

- Give your hand the command to open and see it open.

- Give your hand the command to close and see it close.

Exercise: **Speaking from the Head**

- Maintaining this muscular perspective, say **yes.**
  Notice how yes "feels" when spoken from the head.

- Maintaining this muscular perspective, say **no.**
  Notice how no "feels" when spoken from the head.

Clarity, objectivity, and command are easy to access from the head. If you want more of these qualities, then practice moving from this center. If you are struggling with these issues, then consider exploring this practice to gain more insight and skill. If you already are "too good" at these qualities or spend too much time in this place, then use what you have noticed about the head to recognize when you are here, so you can switch to a different center or perspective.

> *Do you normally perceive and act from your head center?*
>
> *Do you need to develop it more or do you need to let it go?*
>
> *What did you learn about your habits of action?*
>
> *In order to make the change that you want to make, how do you need to use this center differently?*

Exercise: **Moving from your Head in Daily Life**

- At any point, in any action, pause and
  let your face **relax,**
  let your stomach, groin, and lower back **soften,**
  let your attention move **up** to your eyes and ears,
  and from this place, **straighten** your spine
  to let a brand new **breath** emerge with **"Ah ha!"**

- Now re-enter the action.

As you continue in this practice, your ability to consciously access the power of the head will grow. **Over time, the energy of awareness will permeate your life and actions.**

MOVING FROM THE HANDS

The hands are the center of your tactile senses. With your hands, you can touch that which is close to you. The messages that come through touch can easily be overwhelmed by the intensity of your visual and auditory senses. By cultivating this perceptual channel, it becomes much easier to stay in touch with what is going on around you (with your physical hands) and within you (with your mind's hand).

Exercise: **Moving from the Hands**

- **Find your hands.**

  Use your tactile senses to feel what you are touching.

  Notice the pressure and the contact between it and your hands.

  Take a breath and exhale, saying, "Ohhh."

  Use this new energy to soften your chest and your groin.

- Move your hands in the simple rhythm of opening and closing.

- Imagine, as you open your hands, *that "you" are expanding into the world.*

- Imagine, as you close your hands, *that "you" are shrinking back into yourself.*

- As you continue the movement, shift your attention to your chest.

- Let the opening of the hands yield a sense of expansion in the chest *as though the muscles that connect and bind the ribs have become a translucent window that allows "life" to pass through with ease.*

- Let the closing of the hands
yield a subtle tightening of your chest
so that the window becomes a solid door sealing the passageway
between what is outside of you and what is inside.

As your hands and chest open,
expressing your feelings becomes easy.

As your hands and chest close,
it is the time to be with what you feel.

Exercise: Speaking from the Hands

- Maintaining this muscular perspective, say **yes.**
Notice how yes "feels" when spoken from the hands.

- Maintaining this muscular perspective, say **no.**
Notice how no "feels" when spoken from the hands.

Compassion, sensitivity, and feeling in touch with what is going on are easy to access from the hands. If you want more of these qualities, then practice moving from this center. If you are struggling with these issues, then consider exploring this practice to deepen your perception and skill. If you already are "too good" at these qualities or spend too much time in this place, then use what you have noticed about the hands to recognize when you are here so you can switch to a different center or perspective.

Do you normally perceive and act from your hands?

Do you need to further develop your hands' sense
or do you need to pay attention to it less?

What did you learn about your habits of action?

In order to make the change that you want to make,
how do you need to use this center differently?

Exercise: Moving from your Hands in Daily Life

- At any point, in any action, pause and
  let your face **relax,**
  let your stomach, groin, and lower back **soften,**
  let your attention move **out** to your hands,
  and from this place, **straighten** your spine
  to let a brand new **breath** emerge with **"Ohhh ..."**
- Now re-enter the action.

As you continue in this practice, your ability to consciously access the power of the arms and hands will grow. **Over time, the energy of relationship will permeate your life and actions.**

MOVING FROM THE FEET

The feet are the center of your movement senses. With them, you can step out into the world. Having access to the power of the legs, you can absorb and ground the pressures and stresses from your encounters. By cultivating this perceptual channel, it becomes much easier to know that you have the strength to support and sustain yourself no matter what is going on around you.

Exercise: Moving from the Feet

- **Find your feet.**

  Feel them touching the floor.

  Relax your face and mouth.

  Let your shoulders drop.

  Take a breath and exhale, saying, "Ahhhh."

  Soften your belly.
- Move your hands in the simple rhythm of
  opening and closing.

- Pause with your hand in the midst
  of the movement of opening.

- Let your face relax *and take a breath,*
  soften your stomach, groin, and lower back
  and take a breath, and
  let your weight sink to your feet *and take a breath.*

- Return to the rhythm of the simple movement.

- Pause with your hand in the midst of
  the movement of closing.

- Let your face relax *and take a breath,*
  soften your stomach, groin, and lower back
  and take a breath, and
  let your weight sink to your feet *and take a breath.*

Exercise: Speaking from the Feet

- Maintaining this muscular perspective, say **yes.**
  Notice how yes "feels" when spoken from the feet.

- Maintaining this muscular perspective, say **no.**
  Notice how no "feels" when spoken from the feet.

Stability, strength, and movement are easy to access from the feet. If you want more of these qualities, then practice moving from this center. If you are struggling with these issues, then consider exploring this practice to gain more insight and skill. If you already are "too good" at these qualities or spend too much time in this place, then use what you have noticed about the feet to recognize when you are here, so you can switch to a different center or perspective.

Do you normally perceive and act from your feet?

Do you need to further develop your ability to sense with your feet or do you need to pay attention to it less?

What did you learn about your habits of action?

In order to make the change that you want to make, how do you need to use this center differently?

Exercise: Moving from Your Feet in Daily Life

- At any point, in any action, pause and
  let your face **relax,**
  let your stomach, groin, and lower back **soften,**
  let your attention move **down** to your feet,
  and from this place, **straighten** your spine
  to let a brand new **breath** emerge with "**Ahhh ...**"

- Now re-enter the action.

As you continue in this practice, your ability to consciously access the power of the legs and feet will grow. **Over time, the energy of groundedness will permeate your life and actions.**

MOVING WITH ALL OF YOU

Presence is dynamic and creative. Unfortunately, most of us have learned to limit our energy, our abilities, and our possibilities. To become the person we can be requires a shift in our habits of presence. Your personal action habits represent only a small set of what is possible. They are your current favorites, the actions that you use the most.

Action unfolds out of presence. Presence is shaped by action. The person you wish to become does not have the same habits as does the present-day you. The person you wish to become does not perceive the same world that you see now.

Your whole body is a generator and a storehouse for the full range of your potential actions and responses. There is a very big and important difference between the bureaucracy and the whole. When you bring forth a new action from the whole of you, it is more vibrant, creative and appropriate than any habitual action. By working with the exercises in this chapter, you will enhance your natural ability to find the whole of you, at any moment, in any action.

8

KNOWING WITH
YOUR WHOLE BODY

WE HAVE USED the whole body exercises to discover more about where we are now, in other words, what our current habits of action are. You can use the same skills to discover a fuller answer to the crucial question, *what do I want to change?*

It is often said that we already know the answers to our most important questions. Assuming that this is so, where are they hiding? We may know, but they are not in the place that we are looking. We look where we have always looked, the same place where we always act and react from.

**The answers that lead to new ways of being in the world
are not going to be found in the old places,
otherwise we would have already found them.**

The next exercises will assist you in noticing the other (perhaps quieter or less aggressive) answers that are waiting for your attention. In order to hear these profound and powerful answers, use this method:

- Pause.

- Use Centered Presence to release the hold of the old answers.

- Have a paper and pen ready to catch the "quieter" answers before they vanish.

An enhanced body awareness can serve as a doorway to enhanced self-knowledge. Your body contains all that you know. Your filters only allow a small part of what you know to emerge into awareness. This exercise bypasses the usual filtering mechanism allowing you to access more of what you know.

Now use this method to ask the question, *what do I want to change?* Or substitute any question or issue that is currently important to you.

We will repeat the same practice for each of the three major centers of perception. The steps of the exercise are

1. identify an important question

2. focus on the particular center of perceptual orientation

3. listen for the "answers"

4. reflect on what you have learned

Exercise: Knowing from the Head

- **Pause** … in the midst of reading or thinking.

- **Find your head.**

   Use your eyes and look to see where you are.

   Use your ears and listen to what is being said.

   Notice how your head balances on the top of the spine.

   Take a breath and exhale, saying, "Ah ha!"

   Use this new energy to straighten up.

   Take the time for your muscles to shift and your mood to alter.

- Without losing the feeling associated with the head center, **ask yourself the question:** *What do I want to change?*

- **Wait,** giving yourself the time to listen for and hear the answer.

   Let it cook, give it time to unfold.

- Write down the answer and **consider** its meaning for you.

Exercise: **Knowing from the Hands**

- **Pause** ... in the midst of reading or thinking.
- **Find your hands.**

  Use your tactile senses to feel what you are touching.

  Notice the pressure and the contact.

  Take a breath and exhale, saying, "Ohhh."

  Use this new energy to soften your chest and your groin.
- Without losing the feeling associated with the hands center, **ask yourself the question:** *What do I want to change?*
- **Wait,** giving yourself the time to listen for and hear the answer.

  Let it cook, give it time to unfold.
- Write down the answer and **consider** its meaning for you.

Exercise: **Knowing from the Feet**

- **Pause** ... in the midst of reading or thinking.
- **Find your feet.**

  Feel them touching the floor.

  Relax your face and mouth.

  Let your shoulders drop.

  Take a breath and exhale, saying, "Ahhhh."

  Soften your belly.
- Without losing the feeling associated with the feet center, **ask yourself the question:** *What do I want to change?*
- **Wait,** giving yourself the time to listen for and hear the answer.

  Let it cook, give it time to unfold.
- Write down the answer and **consider** its meaning for you.

KNOWING WITH THE WHOLE BODY

You now have four answers to the question, *"what do I want to change?"* In addition to your usual answer, you now know what your head, hands, and feet think about the situation.

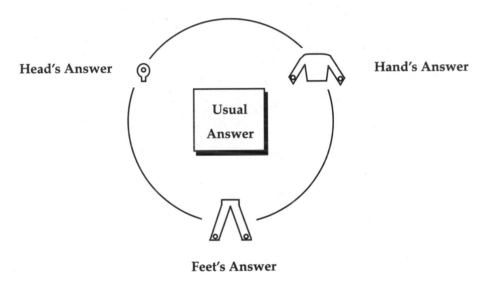

Figure 8–1.

The next step is to bring them together to extract the practical essence of this question.

Exercise: Finding the Integrative Answer

- **Return to Centered Presence.**
  Find your feet ... hands ... head ... breath ...

- **Every few breaths, shift your focus from one center to another.**

  For example, tune into the head and remember to allow the up movement to lift your spine, or tune into the hands and remember to allow the out movement to reach through your hands, or tune into the feet and remember to allow the down movement to sink into the ground through your feet.

• **Shift back and forth between the question and Centered Presence.**

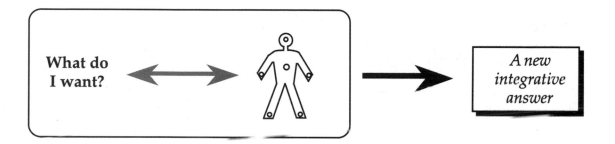

What do I want?

A new integrative answer

Figure 8–2.

What you do with your answer is up to you!

9

PRACTICING FOR SUCCESS

**The only thing more painful than learning from experience
is *not* learning from experience.**

EVEN THE MOST powerful learning can fade rapidly as soon as we leave
the learning environment. It is frustrating to invest so much effort only
to see it evaporate in a short period of time. The concept of learning
decay suggests that if we fail to reinforce and remind ourselves immediately after the learning process, a rapid drop-off of retention is experienced.

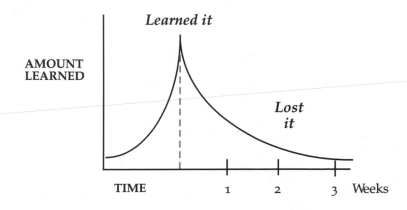

Figure 9–1.

Practice reverses the entropy of learning decay. Not only do you retain more of what you learned, you also build upon your experience and discover even more.

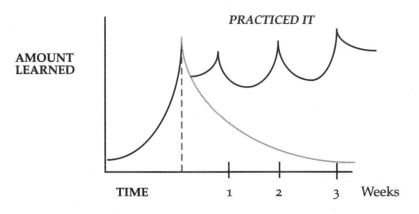

Figure 9–2.

In the early stages of the process of learning, change involves carrying out an activity against the weight of our habits. Unless we strongly support the new behaviors when the learning is still fresh and vibrant, the old habits will win. The last hundred years of research about learning concludes that

- habits are hard to change

- under stress it is easy to revert to old habits

- when they fail to keep their promises to change, people blame and judge themselves harshly

Habits cannot be thrown out the window. They have to be coaxed down the stairs one step at at time.

—Mark Twain

We each learn differently. Learning is complex. Our success in learning varies with the situation, skills required, and number of experiences involved. Some learn best alone and some do better learning with other people. Throughout the book, we have explored the question of why it is hard to change habits and how we revert to old patterns. Our body seeks the familiar neuromuscular pattern or groove. Our bureaucracy wants to keep things as it is.

To change your habits, it is advisable to develop a consistent practice regimen.

PRACTICING FOR SUCCESS

The Vision   *You can be intentionally versatile.*

The Strategy   *To utilize Centered Presence as a foundation for the progressive cultivation of your inherent ability to be both responsive and creative.*

The Process   *To strengthen your ability to stay centered and present independent of external situations or circumstances, in any emotional state, whether positive or negative, and in any particular style of encounter*

The first major limiting factor to achieving our goal is our perceptual and action bias. Our first step is, therefore, to make Centered Presence a new habit. With the material that we have covered thus far, you know enough to install this new habit. At the end of the book, we summarize the essential exercises to deepen and expand the scope of your ability to apply Centered Presence in every aspect of your life.

To establish a workable plan it is necessary to utilize the basic mechanics of habit installation. To develop a new action habit, you have to

1. **create sufficient repetition**
   (reflection and enactment)

2. **practice in a diversity of settings**
   (for example, home, office, public settings)

3. **practice with differing levels of emotional intensity**
   (for example, calm, frustration, anger; with important clients, family)

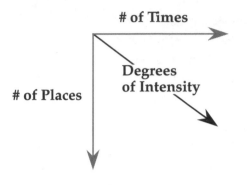

Figure 9–3.

By having repeated experiences in diverse settings with varying degrees of emotional importance and intensity, you can carve a new neuromuscular groove. The ability to utilize your new skills in a variety of complex situations is a measure of the robustness of your learning.

The generic recommendation is to begin your practice in low-risk settings. You can gradually increase your practice to settings which are still low risk but have greater work gain associated with them (for example, meetings with staff members). The next step is to escalate the practice to settings that are higher risk and higher gain (such as clients, customers, or important business partners).

Four simple steps that will support the effectiveness of your practice plan are

1. make realistic goals

2. monitor and record your practice activity

3. create time to reflect on what you have learned

4. share your learning experiences with a buddy

EMBODY CENTERED PRESENCE IN ONE MONTH

Find . . . your feet
. . . your hands
. . . your head
. . . your breath

Questions for Reflection

What situations or internal experiences cause you to lose Centered Presence?

Which is the most difficult body part to remember? The easiest?

In what situations is it difficult to remember Centered Presence? The easiest?

What shifts in your experience, actions, or responses when you do Centered Presence?

Week 1: Home

- Concentrate on those activities associated with home (for example, waking, cleaning, eating, playing, driving, or going to work)

- Focus on specific, frequent actions such as
    picking up the phone
    standing up and walking to get something
    sitting down and eating a meal
    preparing food
    thinking about an upcoming meeting
    standing in line at the store

The test is to bring all of myself into all my actions.

Week 2: Organizing Your Work

- Concentrate on those activities associated with organizing your work (for example, thinking, planning, writing, working on your computer, scheduling)

- Focus on specific, frequent actions such as
    writing down appointments
    talking on the phone
    writing a memo

decision making or brainstorming
packing your briefcase

- Establish a solid foundation of practice before going on to the next "riskier" area

Week 3: Work

- Concentrate on those activities associated with being at work

- Focus on specific, frequent actions such as
consulting with team or staff
attending meetings
problem solving
making presentations
resolving conflicts
meeting with clients
coaching or supervising

Week 4: Your Whole Life

- Concentrate on any and all of your life activities: work, home, and the transitions between them

- Keep in mind that the goal is to maintain Centered Presence regardless of the circumstances

THE SEVEN STEPS
TO SUCCESSFUL PRACTICING

Step 1: *Work with the two sides of practice: reflection and enactment.*

- Reflect and review what you learned
- Enact the behaviors that comprise the learning

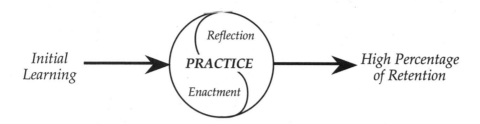

Figure 9–4.

Reflection and review without enactment leaves you uncertain about how well you would respond in real circumstances. Enactment without reflection leads to a tendency to forget the key concepts or issues. Both are necessary to maximize the value of your efforts.

Step 2: *Practice frequently enough to support your learning.*

Enactment: Recent studies suggest that a three-week period is critical for retention. It appears to be the minimal time frame needed to install a new habit or to not let it slip from awareness. Three weeks of consistent practice is sufficient time to lay down the new neuromuscular grooves. If we have not reinforced and recreated the desired behavior within a 15-to-21-day period, the learning almost disappears. It may be buried within but it does not surface on a consistent basis.

**If you genuinely intend to make a change,
then you have to practice.**

Inconsistent practice leads to inconsistent results.

Reflection: Tony Buzan, a best-selling author who writes about human learning, has popularized the concept of review patterns. There are two complementary components that make up a review pattern—frequency and strategy. Frequency refers to how often you bring the newly learned material to awareness. Strategy refers to how you think over the key points. The goal is to trace the critical components in your mind till you are certain they are clear. What is *not* clear should be restudied until you are confident about your understanding. Our suggestion would be to establish the following timing cycle

1. one hour after learning

2. at the end of the first day of learning

3. at the beginning and end of the second day after learning

4. at the end of the first week after learning

5. at the end of the second week after learning

This is not the only timing pattern that works, but it supports the critical three-week action learning period. However, any number of strategic approaches that reflect consistency of effort will yield acceleration of learning retention. Ask yourself what review pattern works best for your circumstances.

What should you think about when you review your learning? Focus on the issues that relate to your goals. The following questions will help the reflection process:

> *What are the most important ideas?*
>
> *How do they apply to my work and life?*
>
> *Do I already use these key ideas?*
>
> *Who are good models of these behaviors?*
>
> *How would I perceive and act differently*
> *if I held these new ideas to be true?*

Review patterns are allies and are not meant to be a burden. They are malleable structures you use to focus the frequency of your reflection and consideration of the salient issues. If "structure" is a major trigger of your resistance, then create a flexible approach that supports a review cycle.

Without a systematic approach, there is a high likelihood of learning decay. The combination of enactment plus reflection (whether structured or flexible) is the best strategy for personal learning retention.

Your success at learning is even greater when there is community or team support to reinforce the recently acquired skills or behaviors. Taking the opportunity to assist a team member in achieving his or her goals has a significant impact on team values and culture.

Step 3: *Observe what you have done in the past to undercut or support change efforts.*

Your previous efforts and their results have shaped your beliefs about your ability to make changes. Do your beliefs support or sabotage your capacity to change? Here are some important questions to consider.

> What are the reasons I use to explain how I have broken my commitments?
>
> Why have my plans for change not succeeded?
>
> What are my beliefs about my ability and strength to change?
>
> What has facilitated my ability to change the most?

Step 4: *Don't get stuck in your image of perfection; do what you can!*

Nothing is more frustrating than having a genuine desire to achieve a goal and yet being unable to achieve it. To expect to change everything overnight is unrealistic. However, you can support your efforts by

- envisioning clear goals
- making a realistic and practical plan
- making an honest contract with yourself

Goals: The clearer you envision the desired outcome the easier it is to steer your actions, thoughts, or feelings in the direction of your intention. As an experienced sailor might say, if you don't know which direction you are headed, then any wind is the right one. When you have a clear sense of either your goal or the strategic direction, an informed choice is possible.

**Fuzzy goals yield unclear results, which in turn
minimize accountability and maximize escape routes.**

You need to recognize what you want to accomplish. Your goals should be yours. No one can tell you what you must do. Choose goals that excite and satisfy your sense of power, relationship, and accomplishment. If you are honest in your self-assessment, you can begin wherever you are and make steady progress. Self-deception about your starting point can only confuse your real progress.

Plan: The most common mistake in the change process is to make an unrealistic plan. Trying to accomplish everything you need to learn in a day is impossible. A plan needs to be consistent with the realities of your whole life. Consider what level of effort and attention you can truly give. Some people discover they schedule themselves for 28 hours a day worth of activities and complain how they "can't get everything done."

Create a simple plan first and then increase the level of challenge after you experience initial success. It is much better to plan small and succeed than to plan big and do nothing. Success can be built upon the prior success. Choose a level of commitment that fits your lifestyle.

Build a strategy that combines the elements of repetition (number of times practiced), diversity of situation (work, home, recreation, and so on), and degree of risk (from low to high). Your plan should include

- **what** I'm practicing
- **when** I'm doing it
- **where** I will be
- **how much** time I'm practicing
- **with whom** am I practicing
- **how frequently** I'm doing it
- **over what time** period or duration am I committed

Training strategically will deepen your ability to access your versatility throughout your life.

It's the commitment to the commitment that counts.

Honesty: To recognize what you want is the first step in getting there. To consider what sacrifices you are willing to make to achieve your desire is the second step. To establish what effort you are willing to give to make it all happen is the third. Lack of honesty about these areas will seriously hamper your progress.

Many of us struggle under the burden of high expectations and little room for forgiveness. If your expectations are inconsistent with your real level of effort, there will be huge gaps between your dreams and your results. Be truthful with where you are and where you want to go. It lightens the psychological load and avoids defensiveness. You can't be other than where you are. It is unworkable to pretend to be somewhere you are not. This breeds self-protection, false fronts, and anxiety.

> *Whether you say you can or say you can't you are right.*
> —Henry Ford

Studies on "the expectation effect" suggest that people achieve their belief, not their capacity. The observer's mind-set or expectation influences his or her assessment of the quality of the work done. Self-esteem and belief are prime determinants in your self-assessment of the value and quality of your work.

**Set your sights high, keep your feet on the ground,
and be clear on what motivates you to make the effort.**

Memory: Forgetting and remembering are natural parts of the cycle of learning. When we forget, there is a tendency to be highly self-critical. The challenge is to forgive yourself for the natural and unavoidable act of forgetting. Self-forgiveness is essential to reduce the negative charge that arises when we slip from our promises. To avoid the negative cycle of despair and self-judgment, forgive yourself when you forget.

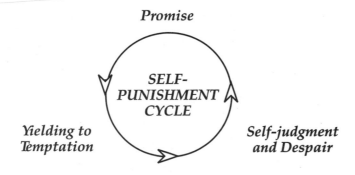

Figure 9–5.

121

This is not giving in to continuing unconsciousness, but an act of self-compassion. We cannot be perfect. Further, if we "punish" ourselves for forgetting with self-criticism, then we anchor the sequence in which awareness of forgetting leads to such criticism. If we praise ourselves for the act of noticing that we forgot, we accelerate our likelihood of noticing again.

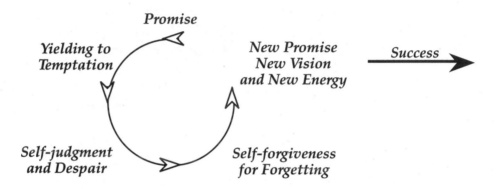

Figure 9–6.

Using Centered Presence to Break the Cycle of Self-punishment

When you realize that you are feeling self-judgment and despair:

Find your feet   This will ground you in the "here and now" and give you the strength to resist the pull of the negative voices and feelings.

Find your head   Using the "Ah ha" breath, lift yourself above the morass of negativity, take a fresh breath, and constructively reexamine the situation.

Find your hands   This will reawaken your sense of being in touch with yourself and the world, and it will strengthen your natural capacity for self-forgiveness.

Acknowledgement: We change both for ourselves and for the world. Some people find praise harder to receive than criticism. They deny any appreciation of their efforts or success. Accept acknowledgment from those around you. To deny support is to ignore feedback that your actions make a difference. Notice what issues surface when you are appreciated or acknowledged. If the issues sabotage your beliefs about success, stop and reflect, *"Isn't that interesting."* From that relaxed and detached place, allow yourself to hear the input without reacting.

Fun: Success in life depends upon our ability to learn. We learn faster when we have fun. So have fun and make a game out of self-discovery. Learning is one of the great joys of life. The whole of you is not afraid to learn. It is at the core of our human heritage to inquire, reflect, make meaning, and transcend our prior level of thinking and functioning. As human beings, we have the opportunity to go beyond the limits of our understanding. Enjoy the adventure. To resist learning and change is to resist life.

Step 5: *Create support.*

> We get by with a little help from our friends.
>
> —John Lennon and Paul McCartney

Your environment can be a great support, a great hindrance, or indifferent to your efforts. Typically, it makes a positive difference if you experience support. If cheerleading does not naturally exist in your life and work situation, consider developing a "buddy" relationship.

A **buddy** is a partner who is 100 percent in support of your success. Buddies may work on similar learning areas or they may not. Their intent is to support your work on your goals even if they are not pursuing similar issues. Early-morning joggers attest to the power of a buddy to help overcome inertia. It is unacceptable to leave your partner waiting on the corner at 6 A.M., so we leave our warm bed and exercise. Without our partner, inertia and a chilly world might derail our weak early-morning intent.

Pick a buddy who is strong enough to cheer you on when your own will and spirit flags. Choosing a buddy who doesn't "walk her talk" is not a help. Ideally, a buddy is either a positive role model or a partner who is also working on her issues.

Identifying **positive role models** is extraordinarily valuable. They embody the qualities that we desire. They show how to get things done by their actions. They make our goals doable because we see it being done. Taking time to talk with positive role models about their skill or actions is a rich learning opportunity. Embarrassment or shyness often arises in such moments because fears of inadequacy surface. Yet most individuals want to share their gifts and appreciate the acknowledgment that comes with being asked about their talents.

Step 6: *Track your progress.*

Feedback is the breakfast of champions.

—Thomas Monson

Monitoring System: The tracking process is crucial to the achievement of our goals. Feedback can accelerate changes in performance. The greater the feedback, the greater the opportunity to correct your course and enhance results. We recommend that you create a simple monitoring system or check sheet to track your practice. Research suggests that tracking your progress over time on charts or graphs can enhance your learning. Manufacturing facilities report that performance increases when people can see their progress.

Daily Review: A basic way to institute and support a tracking process is to develop a daily review. This can be done at the end of the work day or prior to retiring for the night. The daily review can be used to assess what you have done, where you have not stayed on target, and what forces might be working against your completions. You can also examine what supports your efforts. Consider what you can do to decrease the strength of things that interfere with your commitment.

With the daily review, new resolve and strategic focus can be adopted for the next day and you can ascertain whether additional "buddy" support is necessary. It is a strategic checkpoint for your next steps and an opportunity to reflect on what you have just completed.

Public Stance: Public commitments increase our allegiance to our goals. When we "put the stake in the ground" before our friends, colleagues, or family, it has a positive effect upon goal-oriented behavior. We don't want to let our friends down or have their opinion of us decline. They become our community of witnesses, acknowledging our desire to reach to the next level. The realism of our commitment can be sensed by our witnesses. It tempers undue enthusiasm within you and clarifies where you really stand. It encourages us to speak our deepest truth.

Step 7: *Just do it—with awareness!*

The advertising slogan mentality of "Just do it" is seductively simple. But if "doing it" is more of the same action, then doing more of it will not really help. The challenge is to work smarter, not just harder. We do need to break the inertia of "not doing," but we also need to create momentum for *right* action, not just any action. Even small amounts of practice with right action is important.

Little changes can make a big difference in the long run. The principle of continuous improvement has been central to the Total Quality movement in worldwide manufacturing. Continuous improvement supports the view of the big picture through individual actions. One step at a time, we install the components of a new system. One improvement at a time we raise our ability to handle an issue. Each day we train for the goal in each action.

The corollary to continuous improvement is mindfulness in action. By bringing awareness to each and every step, we are centered and present in response to all we encounter. By paying attention throughout the day to the strategic keys that support versatility, we generate a momentum that encourages it to emerge naturally in our daily actions.

**Perceiving and acting from the whole of myself,
I move powerfully in the world.**

THE INNER GAME
OF CHANGE

THE BUREAUCRACY OF habit has a place in our lives similar to the place an operating system, such as DOS or UNIX, has in a computer. Without an operating system, the various application programs cannot run. Making a small change in the operating system programming will affect how everything works.

However, in a living system, making changes is not that easy. We cannot simply add another computer disk with a new and improved way of doing things. For us, the operating system and the user are not separate. The instructions are encoded in our nerves, muscles, and organs. To change successfully means changing at every level of the system.

The human operating system is part of our evolutionary biological heritage. All animals have systems. The difference between the human being and all other animals is that when the human baby is born, there is a greater percentage of the operating system that is left unwritten; it is not hardwired or preprogrammed for action.

Let us take as an example the action of reaching. When a baby is born, the possible set of ways of reaching is relatively unlimited. When the time comes to acquire the skill of reaching, the infant does so in a particular mood, from a particular position, using a particular set of muscles. The baby does this embedded in a social environment with its distinctive set of verbal and nonverbal influences.

The first actions in an untouched/unused field leave the greatest impression. Once the bureaucracy of the nervous system has at least one way to perform a basic action, it is satisfied and does not need to learn more ways of doing it. Progressively, the basic human actions of moving and interacting with the world are acquired. At this point, the bureaucracy solidifies in regards to this action and learning shifts to developing skills in other realms.

Therefore, whenever you "reach" (whether physically, emotionally, or cognitively), some variation of the habitual operating system version of reaching is used. No matter what the application or situation, it is influenced by the first reaching, the earliest learning and patterning.

Imagine that the bureaucracy of the nervous system has been programmed so that reaching is done right-handed, with the arm swinging outward to the side. Therefore, to reach straight ahead requires another layer of action that brings the hand to the left in order to compensate. The simple act of reaching has become layered with compensation upon compensation. The apparently simple act has become complex, unwieldy, and inefficient.

Add to this the fact of the emotional dimension that intertwines with the physical movement. Imagine that reaching was learned while the child was in a mood of frustration and neediness. Subsequently, as an adult, the individual has difficulty in simply reaching for what he or she wants without a background mood of frustration. You can discover the emotions that are inseparable from your actions by experimenting with your own habits of reaching. You can use the protocol we created in the exercises of opening and closing your hand from different perspectives to invent your own practice.

Figure III–1.

In summary, whatever the action—whether internal and subtle, like breathing, or external and obvious, like talking, walking, or writing—your current action habits are built upon layers of early learning. Without attention to these, real change is difficult.

Change seems to be a mysterious process. You look around to take your bearings and then go about your activities. When you look again, the world is different. While at its core, change is mysterious, it is still a natural process. Although each change is different, the basic principles are the same, no matter what the particular circumstances. There is a whole range of intermediary steps that you pass through as you shift from one way of being to another.

The process of changing from one way of being and acting to another way requires the coordination of three related and different types of internal action. We have called these **letting go of what is no longer needed, keeping what is important and adding on what is missing.**

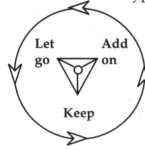

These internal actions of change are not sequential, in other words, it's not that we first let go, then we keep, and then we add on. Each of these actions is going on **all of the time.** At different times, one of them predominates. They are all necessary if a change is going to "stick" or even happen.

Figure III–2.

**Letting go triggers
fear of loss, endings, surrender, and defeat.**

**Keeping triggers
issues of identity, possessiveness, and self-esteem.**

**Adding on triggers
issues of impatience, coordination, and cooperation.**

**The ever shifting dynamic balance between these three actions
creates the ground for change.**

Change requires that you reorganize the pattern of tension that holds your habits into place. The following chapters provide an alternative, user-friendly view of the difficult issues of relaxation and the effective use of effort. We have designed a series of experiments that

1. introduce a new way of looking at the dynamics of change, tension, and effort

2. promote a greater understanding and ability to use the energy of intention and desire

3. teach you how to deepen your ability to relax in the midst of action

10

A USER-FRIENDLY
GUIDE TO LETTING GO

WHENEVER ONE INTERNAL action becomes overly important, problems soon appear. Too much of a concern with **letting go** can generate a slide into a mystical-like passivity and a loss of motivation and drive. Too much of a concern with **adding on** builds layer upon layer of new ideas or quick fixes that have neither depth nor endurance. Too much of a concern with **keeping** promotes the maintenance of the past and makes change itself impossible.

The undervaluing of any one of these internal actions will also engender very real problems. Not enough **letting go** produces a build-up of tension and internal clutter. Not enough **adding on** encourages your dreams to remain just dreams. Not enough **keeping** erodes your sense of center and authenticity.

These issues are not new. There has been much written about these actions of change. So instead of restating what is already well recognized, we are going to emphasize the lesser known, bodily side of change.

Of the three internal actions of change, letting go seems to have the greatest emotional charge. We are told this is the secret to change, yet even thinking about it can produce waves of fear and confusion. It is very true that letting go is much easier to say than to do.

Much of the energy and emotion associated with this simple action is a direct result of the commonly held belief that **letting go** means letting go of *everything*. However, that is not what it really means.

Letting go means releasing that which is no longer needed so that

you can be where you are now. It is a series of small actions. Letting go of everything *is* impossible. You can say it, but the integrity of your body will resist it. To appreciate the real difference between the two beliefs, say to yourself:

> • "**Letting go** *means letting go of* everything."
>
> Notice how your muscles, feelings, and thoughts shift in response to this belief.
>
> • "**Letting go** *means releasing that which is no longer needed to be where I am now.*"
>
> Notice how your muscles, feelings and thoughts shift in response to this belief.

As long as you hold onto the belief that "letting go means letting go of *everything*," then the defense forces of both your bureaucracy and your biological self will combine to resist your desires for change.

There is another commonly held belief about **letting go** that makes it more difficult than it needs to be. This is the belief that it should be easy to just "let go," "open up," or "release the negative tensions." Given this belief, we are continually shocked, frustrated, disappointed, and depressed about the possibility of ever really letting go. We want it to be a complete experience, where all the tension we hold deep inside dissipates and we are left free and relaxed.

If the tension you want to release was formed in one contractive movement, all at once, then it could be released, all at once, in one expansive movement. The letting go would release the pressure and you would expand, refreshed and empowered, back into the world.

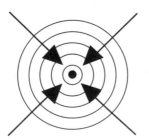 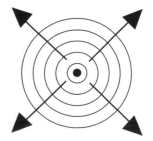

Figure 10–1.

However, the habitual pressure and tension that you experience did not happen all at once. It is the product of many contractions, each different, that occurred over a long period of time. While it feels like a solid mass of tension, it is not. It is more like a knot that was formed by layer upon layer of tensing.

a solid mass of tension?   *a layered knot of tensings?*

Figure 10–2.

The action and results of **letting go** are shaped by what you believe. Your methods, expectations, and experiences will be very different depending on whether you call this tension a *mass* or a *knot*.

Letting go *is* like a release of pressure. We got where we are now not by a singular contraction but by many. The knot formed, one contraction at a time, each contraction in response to pressure coming from a different direction. Therefore, the process of release will be the same—a series of many small expansions. Since the timing of the contractions was neither planned nor periodic, neither will be the timing of the releases. The series of releasings that constitute letting go of the past will each emerge from a different place, and will want to move outward with a different direction, speed, and quality.

LETTING GO OF ONLY WHAT YOU DO NOT NEED

The following exercises move from the world of words into the concrete world of action. They help you know **in your body** the difference between letting go of everything and letting go of only what you no longer need. In addition to what you will learn about the muscular relaxation side of letting go, you will also be cultivating the qualities of solidity, groundedness, and calm.

Every encounter, whether in the world or with something bubbling up from within, is a moment of potential change. Every encounter is filled with tension. Your beliefs about tension and change shape both how you experience such encounters and deal with them.

Living in the "old" paradigm of mind versus body, there are two basic choices that one can make. Each choice engenders a whole way of being in the world. Notice your experience as you read these two contradictory statements about tension.

- **Tension is good:** *I can use it to make things happen.*

- **Tension is bad:** *It hinders me in making things happen.*

The movement of change is the continual dance of shifting tensions. Tension is neither good nor bad. It is simply what is so. The question is, *how can I work harmoniously with the tension of life?*

Many people think the key to accomplishment is to "just do it" and then do more of it. The success of this approach depends upon the "it" that you are doing. **Working harder is only valuable if you are working in the "right" way.**

Here is a story that illustrates this point. An older man shuffled into Stuart's office one day. He was depressed, with low self-esteem, and unable to enjoy life. In his youth, he had been a race car driver, a gymnast, and a ballroom dance teacher. I asked him to stand up and sit down, so I could observe him in action. He strained, trying to push himself out of the chair, only to fall back. Have you ever watched someone fail at this simple movement? This could not be good for one's self-confidence.

I realized that he was attempting to stand up using the same method and mechanics that he used when he was a young man. I could imagine him leaping out of the chair into an aerial flip and landing, "ta da!" No wonder he experienced himself as a failure.

I showed him a new way to stand and sit using a more efficient method that substituted precision for brute force. By shifting his weight and using his hands, he was able to find the balance point for easy movement. I showed him a few other simple movements with their accompanying mood and mechanics. I saw him a few weeks later and I can report, without exaggerating, that he bounded up the stairs to my office.

The real issue was not his age or his physical strength. The problem was in his method and in his understanding of effort.

THE POWER OF MOVEMENT

The underemphasis on movement in our culture leads to a serious lack of embodied power among our leaders. One mark of the difference between those who can generalize their learning and those who cannot is an understanding and use of the principles and strategies of movement. **By movement, we do not mean simply moving through space** (for instance, as a dancer or athlete does), **rather we are referring to the way in which we act and behave in the world.**

Other cultures have openly encouraged the development of individual and collective respect for the power of movement and conscious action. For example, if you were to visit China, you would see millions of people, every day, in the parks, moving and practicing movement. It is part of the cultural heritage of the Chinese to enact through movement certain facets of their philosophy and science with the expectation that health benefits will follow.

It would not be uncommon to find a Japanese executive practicing the simple drawing of a sword or the pulling of a bow. That these activities will assist the development of certain mental or spiritual qualities that will "make the difference" in the business world is taken for granted.

Movement is not held in the same light in the Western world. There is a famous story that compares the cultures in this regard. Imagine that we are in fifteenth century Japan. We come upon a small rice and sake shop, and sitting at a table, by himself, is a man eating his meal. His clothes are old and covered with patches, for he is a ronin or masterless samurai. Into the shop come several young samurai, dressed in their exquisite livery. They are very boisterous and filled with the arrogance of youth.

Seeing that this older man has a really beautiful sword, they decide that it is too good for someone who looks so poor. So they begin insulting him, trying to draw him into a fight that they are sure they will win. The older man just ignores them and continues to eat his meal. The weather is hot and the flies ever present. Without seeming to pay any attention to the young punks, and without disturbing his meal, the ronin just reaches up with his chopsticks and pulls several flies out of the air. Witnessing this, the men quickly quiet down, apologize, and leave the inn. They realize that this man is a master of the sword and that they have no chance to win.

Now imagine that we are in the American wild West. Sitting in the saloon is an older man, poorly dressed, eating his meal. Strutting into the bar come several young cowhands from one of the big ranches. Seeing that this drifter has a beautiful pair of guns, they begin insulting him, trying to draw him out into a fight. The man ignores them and continues eating. The weather is hot and the flies ever present. Without seeming to pay any attention to the young punks, and without disturbing his meal, the man just reaches up and pulls several flies out of the air. Witnessing this, the men say, "So what if you can grab flies, how good are you with a gun?"

This is the difference in attitude concerning movement. In Japan, a swordsman who could not do beautiful calligraphy was not considered to be a really excellent swordsman. To gain skill in one area and not have it extend to the totality of the person's life was unthinkable and crude. In the West, it often seems to be unimaginable that there should be any carryover at all.

In the gunslinger story, the realm of movement is separate from the rest of one's actions in the world. In the samurai story, movement is viewed as being inseparable from the rest of one's life and is a mirror of the totality of our development.

How I move is a statement of the whole of me.

The way of movement not only deals with the movements of the body but also the movement of the mind. To know the movement of your opponent's mind, study the movement of your own mind.

—Walter Muryasz

11

RELAXATION IN ACTION

LIFE OFFERS US many opportunities for relaxation. Unfortunately, we often wait for the action to be complete before letting go of what we no longer need. Then it is too late in the process for making deep changes. The completion of an action is, of course, an excellent time to release the accumulated tensions from the old actions.

As humorous as it may to sound, there are three times when we need to remember to relax: 1. before the action, 2. in the midst of the action, and 3. after the action.

This chapter will teach you the basic skills you need to take advantage of relaxing both in the midst of your actions and while you are preparing to act. For simplicity's sake, and because they provide an excellent laboratory and training ground, we will to work with the actions of standing and sitting.

Exercise: **Standing and Sitting**

- Stand in front of a chair with your feet spread apart and with the back of your legs touching the chair.

- Maintaining your gaze straight ahead, slowly sit down.

- Maintaining your gaze straight ahead, slowly stand up.

- Repeat several times.

There are many ways to stand and sit. The particular mechanics used in this exercise cultivate a "grounded" quality of presence. As you engage in the movement, you will begin to notice either a calming effect

Figure 11–1.

or the feeling of boredom rising up. Depending upon your history and constitution, one or the other may appear. We ask that you give in to neither.

- When **calm** is overemphasized, **tension** is undervalued.

- When **boredom** is overemphasized, **relaxation** is under-valued.

The concept of tension involves the interplay between the acts of tensing and relaxing. Letting go in the mood of calm often leads to the release of too much tension. In the mood of boredom, very little is either noticed or released. We invite you to explore tension in a dynamic middle zone.

The attitudinal key to this exercise can be summed up in the phrase, **"Moment by moment, I am exactly where I am."** As you stand and sit, and thoughts and feelings rise up wanting to be noticed, acknowledge them and return your attention to the mechanics and muscular moves required for this action. This internal action is important for the cultivation of patience.

Anthony: Session #2

After spending a month practicing the attitude "intention, not feeling, leads action," Anthony reported that he was making real progress. For the first time, he was able to consistently stop himself from getting drawn into other people's stories and feelings. Instead of losing his direction and taking up theirs, he was able to hold his focus and state his message. This inspired him to go for the next step. Anthony realized that even though he was being more decisive in his speaking, he was still being seen as not strong enough. He wanted to handle this issue now.

We designed a two-part program to assist him in cultivating the specific quality of strength that he needed to do his job, but that would not go counter to his "way of being." The first component of his training was built around the everyday action of standing and sitting. However, instead of performing this action in one smooth motion, he had to use a series of four and eight discrete mini-moves to accomplish the task. Each time he stopped, he was to say to himself, "Moment by moment, I am exactly where I am." This statement, when coupled with this particular way of moving, produced in Anthony a sense of personal solidity that over time will strengthen his ability to resist the demands of others.

The second part of Anthony's program was designed to counter his personal bureaucracy's reaction to this new way of operating, being strong and solid. One of the major differences between someone who moves through life as a feeler versus someone who operates with intent, decisiveness, and authority lies in the amount of tension they can tolerate and even enjoy. On the positive side, the ability to hold intensity for long periods of time allows you to push through obstacles and make things happen. On the down side, a high degree of habitual tension acts to close you off from others and makes heartful communication difficult.

Anthony's system was programmed to consider tightness and tension to be negative. As long as he holds being relaxed as better than being tense, he will have a hard time maintaining his new decisiveness and independence. With this in mind, we gave Anthony an exercise based upon *wanting*. His job was to want to stand yet not move and to hold the wanting energy for a period of time beginning with three breaths and working up to one minute. This internal weightlifting exercise will build a new set of muscles, ones that will support him in holding his own position. Anthony realized that this was now the time for "no pain, no gain."

PAUSING IN THE MIDST OF ACTION

The fear of falling is the first reflex reaction that the human infant experiences. It helps shape the foundation layer of your personal bureaucracy. Whenever letting go gets associated with falling, it is automatically labelled a dangerous event by the bureaucracy. By emphasizing a grounded way of moving, you can minimize the effect that your historical fear of falling has on your current behavior.

If you experiment by yourself or watch other people, you will begin to notice that most people actually fall, all or part of the way, into the chair. Falling and sitting are connected in the associative mind of the bureaucracy. If lasting change is the goal, then facing hidden fears is a necessary part of the journey.

The instruction, "stand in front of the chair with your feet spread apart, with the back of your legs touching the chair," which was in the last exercise, reminds your nervous system that where you are headed is close at hand, and that there is no abyss awaiting you. Experiment with this. By continually reminding yourself that you are not going to fall, only sit, you can focus your conscious attention, instead, on the act of bending your legs.

The instruction, "maintaining your gaze straight ahead," is also designed to keep your bureaucracy from thinking about falling. Experiment with this. If you look down and see only the empty space between you and the floor, then you will feel a heaviness that makes this simple act more difficult.

Gazing straight ahead is an internal act that extends your attention outward. The immediate side effect is the possibility of a muscular lengthening of your spine. This redistributes your weight and allows your limbs to do their job, in the most effective way.

The muscular key to this exercise is **keep your weight over your feet.** Let the act of sitting and standing be about the shifting of balance and patterns of tension, and not about just getting up and getting down. Explore the differences.

Exercise: Pausing and Relaxing in the Midst of Action

- Maintaining your gaze straight ahead,
  sit down even more slowly.

- Halfway down, pause.

  Relax your belly, shoulders, and knees.

  Allow a breath.

  Continue sitting until you reach the chair.

- Maintaining your gaze straight ahead, slowly stand up.

- Halfway up, pause.

  Relax your belly, shoulders, and knees.

  Allow a breath.

  Continue standing.

- Repeat several times.

Now that you have the basic mechanics, it is time to explore the idea of **letting go of what is not needed to be where you are.** The first step is to pause, for without this action, letting go will remain just an idea. Pausing is made difficult when it is confused with stopping. Stopping is usually found in the context, "I move. I stop moving." Many active people avoid stopping for fear of or in recognition of the effort involved in getting back into motion.

Pausing is a special kind of stopping. It creates an opportunity to discover the hidden micro-actions that support your external actions.

I stop *in the midst of* the action.
I do not stop the action.

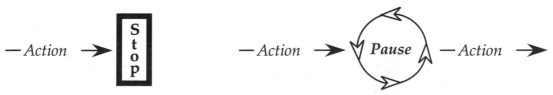

Figure 11–2.

The instructions advise you to pause, half way through the movement, and then to relax your belly, shoulders, and knees. To take this action out of the usual paradigmatic context of physical actions versus mental actions, let's remember why we are doing this. Two basic premises of Retooling on the Run are

1. the bureaucracy of our habits naturally defends itself against change

2. by recognizing and neutralizing these defenses, we can encourage our personal bureaucracy to accept new patterns or programs

Practicing *pausing* develops the muscular strength to rein in the galloping horse called habit. Begin with a simple maneuver and pause half way through the act. Watch out for the defenses. A favorite of many personal bureaucracies is to radiate "negative" feelings, such as "this is boring," "this is stupid," "when do we get to do something fun?"

You probably recognize these tactics. Your bureaucratic defenses tend to use the same predictable reactions no matter what the situation. We are only doing a simple movement. Imagine how easily it can ensnare you when life gets really intense.

The purpose of relaxing your belly, shoulders, and knees is to soften the muscular foundation that supports your verbal and interpersonal behavior. It is much harder for a survival-rooted habit to sustain itself when these body regions are relaxed. When you initiate the letting go process, listen for another round of habit defenses.

Christopher: Session #2

In his last session Christopher was taught the Centered Presence exercise. He discovered that using it enabled him to regain his "rhythm." The next stage of retooling focused on deepening and strengthening his sense of control and purposefulness. As a declared workaholic Christopher didn't know the meaning of the word *stop*. On the positive side, he got a lot done. On the negative side, not stopping had built up a wall of tension that had created its own set of problems.

Even though Christopher was aware of this tension and its side effects, he only knew his old method, which was to work, work, work, and then STOP. After discussing the pros and cons of this operating mode, he expressed a readiness to find a new way of using his energies, one more conducive to health and sanity. The exercise that Christopher learned was deceptively simple. It involved the ordinary activity of standing and sitting, something he did hundreds of times a day. However, instead of just unconsciously standing and sitting, he was asked to stop—right in the middle of the act—and to let go of whatever excess tension he could find. The key was *excess*. He had to keep the necessary tensions.

By stopping or pausing in the midst of the act of sitting, and letting go of only that which he did not need, Christopher was able to learn—with his whole body—that stopping was not the enemy. If that was true, then he could stop more often, even if just for a second. Each time he stopped, he could release some of the built-up tension. With this new rhythm, he could go on for much longer than ever before. By becoming a healthy workaholic, he could satisfy his desire for accomplishment and his need for rest and relaxation.

As an extra bonus, Christopher discovered that when he chose to stop and to let go he found the time to reevaluate the situation, fine-tune his direction, and decide his next step. This opportunity for increased control had been hidden by his fear of stopping.

Exercise: Putting More Pauses in Your Movement

In this exercise, you can explore, in more detail, what you have learned. By moving slower, the hidden insecurities, imbalances, and buried issues become observable.

- Maintaining your gaze straight ahead,
  sit down even more slowly than last time.

- Pause one quarter of the way down and let go of the excess
  tension in your belly, buttocks, legs, face, and shoulders.
  Allow a breath.

- Pause halfway down and let go of the excess tension in
  your belly, buttocks, legs, face, and shoulders.
  Allow a breath.

- Pause three quarters of the way down and let go of the excess tension in your belly, buttocks, legs, face, and shoulders.

  Allow a breath.

- Continue sitting until you reach the chair.

- Return to Centered Presence.

- Now reverse the process and stand up slowly.

- Pause one quarter of the way up and let go of the excess tension in your belly, buttocks, legs, face, and shoulders.

  Allow a breath.

- Pause halfway up and let go of the excess tension in your belly, buttocks, legs, face, and shoulders.

  Allow a breath.

- Pause three quarters of the way up and let go of the excess tension in your belly, buttocks, legs, face, and shoulders.

  Allow a breath.

- Continue until you are standing.

- Return to Centered Presence.

- Repeat several times.

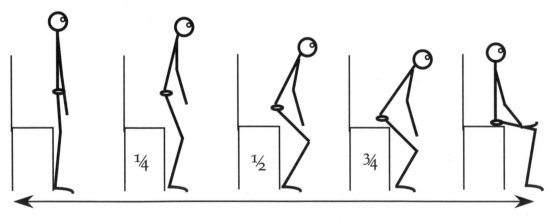

Figure 11–3.

Earlier, we spoke of the two different ways in which letting go can be understood.

- I let go of everything.
- I let go of only what I no longer need.

This exercise takes us to the heart of the conceptual difference. Every time you give yourself the direction to relax, only some of your muscles listen. This is how it is supposed to be. If letting go meant that all of your tension relaxed downward, then you would become a formless blob. This is not the way to be a master of action.

After doing the exercise a number of times, notice if there is a consistent pattern. Which muscles are "agreeable" and able to relax? Which resist the opportunity? As you go through your day, pay particular attention to these body regions. Notice how often they tighten, and in response to which situations or people.

If you find the same muscles tightening in real life as they did during this "safe" experiment, then take a moment to sit or stand. Use this moment as an opportunity to locate and relax the tensions of stress. Then, reenter whatever action in which you are involved.

The more often you pause,
the more often you can release unnecessary tensions.

The more often you pause,
the more often you can begin again.

The more often you pause, the more often you can ask the questions:

> *What do I need to **keep** in order to be where I am now*
> *while at the same time moving toward my envisioned future?*

> *What do I need to **add on** to what I have now*
> *in order to move toward the future?*

When you relaxed your belly, did your spine relax too much, or not enough? When you relaxed your shoulders, did you lose your straight-ahead looking gaze? When you relaxed your knees, did your weight suddenly become much too heavy?

Balanced action requires a fluid coordination between
letting go of tension and keeping tension.

Exercise: Everyday Standing and Sitting

- Slowly and easily sit and stand.

- In the midst of the movement make many **mini-pauses.**

- With each pause remind yourself to
  let go of what you do not need to be where you are now.

- Continue to move and pause and move and pause.

By practicing with slow precision, you can progressively cultivate
the feeling awareness and strength that allows you to make the change
you want. Each time you direct yourself to let go, let it go deep. Allow
yourself time for the muscular movement of relaxation to get started
and build up momentum. Watch for the hard-to-avoid tendency to lose
depth when you increase speed. Rushing through looks a lot like moving fast, but it is very different. Rushing produces shallow results.

By starting slowly and then speeding up and then going slowly
again, you will discover your personal bureaucracy's way of sacrific-
ing depth for time. Recognizing these moments is crucial to your success. As soon as shallow replaces deep in your actions and values, the
pathway to authentic and enduring change grows narrow.

**Without letting go of where we have been,
the future becomes the past extended into the future.**

Letting go is a series of small actions.

**At each moment, pause and let go of
what you no longer need to be where you are.**

THE MANY SIDES OF EFFORT

How you use effort affects your physical and emotional health as well
as your actions. Doctors George Whatmore and Daniel Kohli spent

many years studying the neurophysiology of action using a multi-channel electro-myometrogram (EMMG).[1] They discovered that effort is inherently connected to and affects all aspects of the nervous system, especially:

- *the reticular activating system:* influences the level of organismic arousal

- *the hypothalmus:* influences both the endocrine and autonomic nervous systems

- *the brain stem and spinal cord:* influences signals from the higher brain centers

- *the limbic system:* influences emotions

- *the neocortex:* influences thinking

Effort is wired into the whole system. Whatmore and Kohli proposed that specific patterns of effort made the difference between health and dysfunction. They described four realms of effort.

Bracing effort is when your muscles are partially contracted or "on guard." This is the physiological and biochemical preparation for action. *This is the effort of readiness.*

Representation effort is the bodily activity that produces sensory images (including visual, auditory and proprioceptive images). These representations are central to both thinking and acting. *This is the effort of thinking and believing.*

Attention effort is the bodily activity that focuses our awareness on one signal or input more strongly than another. *This is the effort of focusing and concentrating.*

Performing effort is the bodily activity that yields overt action. *This is the effort of coordinated action.*

Your patterns of effort strongly influence your physiology, your experience and your actions. **The source of both your problems and your successes lies in the quality of your efforts.** The misuse or misdirection of effort yields stress, wear and tear, and reduced capacity for achievement. Doing *more* of the wrong thing does not help you to attain that which you desire. Working harder is only valuable if you are working in the right way. The proper use of effort yields high-quality results with an experience of flow.

THE TENSION OF WANTING

Embedded as we have been in the "old" paradigm of body/mind separation, it is no wonder that **performing effort** has received the most notice. The only way we can retool our habits of action is by expanding our perceptions to include all of the realms of effort. We need to look beneath the surface to see how our habits of attention, representation, and bracing either support or distort the performance of our actions in the world.

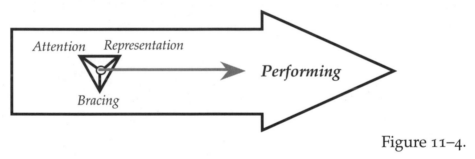

Figure 11–4.

Before you actually move into action, a complex series of internal actions is already underway. As soon as you decide upon or envision a goal, your energies mobilize to accomplish it. The way you mobilize has a profound effect both upon the immediate results and upon the long-term side effects. The way you mobilize is a function of the interplay between the four types of effort.

Mobilizing one's energies for action has been described in many ways. It is often called "intention" or "will" or "wanting." Wanting is a real action, although it is takes place below the normal threshold of perception. As wanting increases in intensity, there is a corresponding response on the energy-muscle level. This build-up of energies can be viewed as the tangible power of wanting.

As an experiment, imagine that there is something that you want to obtain. Now, say to yourself, "I want it." Start with very little intensity in your voice and slowly increase and then decrease it. Notice the muscular tensions, feelings, memories, etc. that rise up to fit the degree of "wanting" that you are using.

I want it.

I want it.

I want it.

I want it NOW!

Wanting stands between you and your goal. Not enough wanting usually leads to not enough doing. Too much wanting produces so much excess tension that the connection between vision and action gets distorted. In other words, it is easy to forget both why you are doing what you are doing and to strategize the best way to get there.

Pauline: Session #2

The first stage in Pauline's retooling adventure was to rediscover the value of having her feet on the ground. Contrary to popular opinion, authentic and lasting change requires that you rebuild your organization from the bottom up. A new vision is merely the starting point. It is easy to be blinded by the intensity of one's vision and miss or devalue the obstacles along the way. With one's feet on the ground, these can become powerful opportunities to demonstrate and to test the workability of your point of view.

As long as her personal bureaucracy was programmed to "keep the energy up," Pauline continued to rush through her work, missing the important details. In her previous attempts to change this habit, she discovered that using willpower to slow down produced a counter response of depression, anxiety, and loss of direction. We decided to take another approach, one that did not directly challenge her system's defenses.

If you were to observe the first instant of action from a whole body perspective, you would discover that the very intention to move is a physical force. The effort of "wanting" engages your muscles. The basic exercise that Pauline learned was to want to stand up and then to let go of the desire. In the first stage of the practice we asked her to stand up part of the way and then sit back down. Progressively she was able to feel how her muscles engaged as she soon as she projected her desire to stand. She discovered very quickly that if she stayed with her vision yet did not move, she could feel just as intense and excited as she did when she flew through her work. The experience of this exercise revealed to Pauline that slowing down did not have to mean losing her drive and energy.

There is much more to *wanting* than we usually consider. Here are several exercises to expand your understanding of this important issue.

Exercise: Wanting to Stand

- Sit back comfortably in your chair.

- Say to yourself, **"I want to stand up."**

- Slowly increase the intensity of your wanting
  until you can feel the muscles
  of your torso, legs, neck, and face straining,
  trying to lift you up off of the chair.

- Now, say to yourself, **"I don't have to get up."**

- Relax back into the chair, releasing the built-up tensions.

- Repeat several times until you can clearly feel
  the tension of wanting.

Sitting in the midst of the tension of wanting to stand yet not moving, it's possible to feel as though there is a wall in the way. When this barrier is considered to be an illusion or the product of self-limiting ideas, then the appropriate response is to push harder, as in, "If at first you don't succeed, try, try again." But what if the barrier is supposed to be there? What then would be the best response?

According to Sir Isaac Newton, an object at rest tends to stay at rest, while an object in motion tends to stay in motion. Whenever you begin to shift from one state, position, or way of being to another, you encounter a barrier to free and easy change. This is called **inertia.** This resistance to change is a part of the innate bureaucracy of nature.

You cannot avoid the physical universe's desire to maintain things the way they are now. The British biologist Rupert Sheldrake suggested that the world has habits, just like we do. On the positive side, the resistance of inertia provides the basic boundaries upon which your sense of self-esteem, integrity, and dignity depend. Without these boundaries, there is no sense of personal identity.

Learning to accept the reality of inertia opens the door to the ability to use it, purposefully and effectively. Wanting, like any other action, has to deal with the law of inertia.

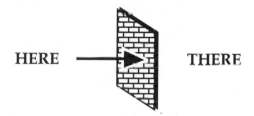

HERE ⟶ THERE

Figure 11–5.

Newton also stated that every action has an equal and opposite reaction. As you "fire up" your intent or wanting energy, the forces of inertia immediately arise to act as a barrier to your action. Pushing through this wall of inertia requires great expenditures of energy. When you push blindly against that which seems to block your way, the intensity of the battle distorts your perceptions. In addition, the path that you saw (before you began your action) is changed by your excess effort.

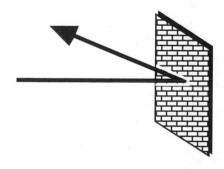

Figure 11–6.

Exercise: Building Up the Wanting

- Sit back in your chair.
- Activate your wanting energy by saying to yourself, "I want to stand up."
- Let it build up until you are almost shaking with the effort.
- Now push through the wall until you are standing.
- Notice your feelings, inner conversations, and tensions.
- Repeat several times.

Since we were not taught about this issue, it is no wonder that we have spent so much of our time and energy over the years struggling and fighting. Change is difficult enough in itself without having to battle so much. What if a large measure of the difficulties that you have faced in trying to change were a function of this unavoidable issue and not solely a function of your lack of will?

In a fight between you and the world, bet on the world.

—Franz Kafka

When you can tell the difference between when you are fighting natural laws and when you are fighting yourself, your odds for success will radically increase. This is one of the real secrets of accomplishment. In order to maximize your use of effort, you have to work with the natural resistance to change. By refusing to fight the unnecessary battles and by accepting the tension of inertia, **you can discover the door that is in the wall** and walk through it to move closer to your goal.

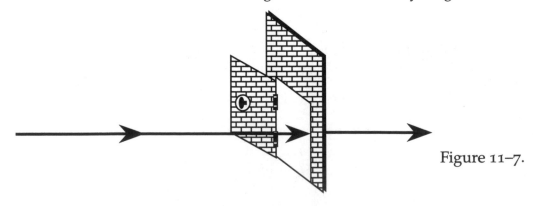

Figure 11–7.

OPENING THE DOOR

It is only when you recognize that you are encountering the wall of inertia that you can transform it into a door. By exploring the tension of wanting in your everyday actions, you will be able to recognize when you are getting stuck trying to break the wall down or ignore its existence.

The wall seems to grow larger and thicker whenever we get so caught up in our goals that we forget both the rest of the world and the rest of ourselves. Conversely, the wall grows thinner and more translucent as we remember the larger field of activity within which we move and experience.

The energy of the tension of wanting has a seductive lure. As its voice grows louder—"I have to have it!"—the signals from the clear heart and mind grow harder to discern. Concern for consequences and/or attention to the most effective means fade by the wayside. It is as though this energy is seeking to find the most direct and shortest pathway to the object of desire.

The energy of desire can easily seduce one away from wholeness and clarity. Wanting is a very powerful force, and therefore it must be treated with respect and caution.

Centered Presence acts like a dynamic anchor, allowing you to stay focused on what you want while at the same time losing neither the world nor yourself. As you hold your whole body in the field of your attention, the energy of wanting spreads to your hands, your feet, and your head. The distortions and intensity dissipate and the way through can be more clearly seen.

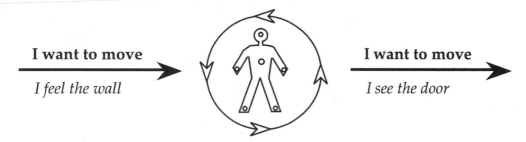

Figure 11–8.

155

Exercise: Wanting and Relaxing into Your Feet

- Sit back in your chair and activate your wanting energy.

- Let it build up until you are almost shaking with the effort.

- Without letting go of the wanting to stand, *find your feet.*

- Gently soften the tension in your torso.

- As you breathe, let the tension and energy of wanting flow down into your legs and toes.

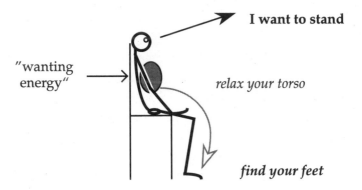

Figure 11–9.

- Continue to breathe as you direct the energy into your feet.

- Slowly but surely use your legs to bring you to standing.

- Repeat several times.

As your torso relaxes and the tension flows into your feet, imagine you can feel a special quality of power growing upward from the floor and filling all of you. It is as though you have found a deeper and more solid place upon which to stand. The wall now feels less substantial, it seems to part or give way as you move upward to standing.

Figure 11–10.

By the time you reach the standing position, you radiate a solid and grounded presence that will be noticed, consciously or unconsciously, by the people you encounter.

The strategy is to shift your attention back and forth between

1. your desire to stand

2. your experience of the wall of inertia

3. the internal actions of relaxing and directing the breath

It is the synergy between these that opens the door. Not enough relaxing and the wall stays solid. Too much relaxing and the desire melts away. *The proper use of relaxation makes all the difference.*

Dorothy: Session #2

In our last session, Dorothy learned that it really *was* possible to combine power and caring. She told us that she spent several weeks practicing this new way of using her hands, breath, and posture in the midst of daily business and personal encounters. She discovered, to her amazement, that when she consciously gestured with her hands, she relaxed, felt less of a need to drive right through her colleagues, and was somehow less afraid. She also reported that whenever she got caught up in "superdrive," tension built up in her eyes, shoulders, and upper back.

Dorothy realized that when she was in superdrive she was assessed by others as being overly aggressive or "a bitch." When she was able to use her new practice "on the run," this assessment did not come up. Since it is not always possible to catch a pattern before it is triggered, we taught Dorothy another exercise designed to transform her aggressive superdrive into being just plain powerful.

"Superdrive" is a side effect of trying to smash through resistance. In Dorothy's case, this strategy was built upon the belief that nothing should stand in the way of her intent or declared goal. There are several factors that she did not take into account. The most important was her lack of understanding of inertia. Whenever you want to shift from being at rest to being in motion, you have to cross "an inertial boundary" or wall of resistance. Given that the systems we work within are filled with people, we can easily project this inherent and appropriate resistance onto people instead, and see them as resisting us. Since this is how Dorothy operated, no wonder she was seen as aggressive and uncaring.

The exercise Dorothy learned began in a similar way to the one we gave Pauline: *want* to stand but don't complete the action. However, in this case, instead of using the strategy of "let go of the tension," we emphasized rechanneling it in another direction. The steps of the exercise were to 1. *want* to stand, 2. don't move and don't release the tension, 3. find your feet, 4. aim the energy down to the floor and use your legs to stand. After doing this, Dorothy felt intensely powerful and in control. When she used this practice in a meeting, she was assessed as serious, powerful yet not overly aggressive.

Exercise: Wanting and Relaxing into Your Hands

- Sit back in your chair and activate your wanting energy.

- Let it build up until you are almost shaking with the effort.

- Without letting go of the wanting to stand, *find your hands*

- Gently soften the tension in your torso.

- As you breathe, let the tension and energy of wanting flow out into your arms and fingers.

I want to stand

relax your torso

find your hands

Figure 11–11.

- Continue to breathe as you direct the energy into your hands.

- Reach forward with your hands and use this momentum to bring you to standing.

- Repeat several times.

As the tension begins to flow from your torso into your hands, you will discover that while the rest of your body is stuck in the chair, your hands are free to move. Aim them in a forward and upward direction, and when your torso begins to move, following the arms, use your legs to complete the motion.

Figure 11–12.

By using your arms to direct the wanting energy, the impenetrable wall becomes an open door. As in fairy tales, whenever you reach out and touch that which you fear, it magically transforms into something beautiful. Moving in this way, you begin to radiate the presence of someone who is unafraid to meet the challenges of relationship.

Exercise: Wanting and Relaxing into Your Head

- Sit back in your chair and activate your wanting energy.

- Let it build up until you are almost shaking with the effort.

- Without letting go of the wanting to stand, *find your head*.

- Gently soften the tension in your torso.

- And as you breathe, let the tension and energy of wanting flow up into your neck and head.

find your head   **I want to stand**

relax your torso

Figure 11–13.

- Continue to breathe
  as you direct the energy into your head.

- Move forward with your head leading
  and use this momentum to bring you to standing.

Figure 11–14.

- Repeat several times.

As soon as the torso begins to soften and the energy flows upward into your neck and head, it is as though you (the conscious perceiver and actor) have been released. Lifted above the struggle between the wanting and the wall, you can more clearly see your goal and reaffirm your desire to reach it.

Using what you discovered in the last exercise with your hands, now your head is free to move. Pretend that your head is a hand and stretch it forward and up along the path of standing. Let the tension begin to spread down the spine, first to the neck, and then down your back. What you are feeling is the spine mobilizing itself for action. When your weight is over your feet, use your legs to stand. Moving in this way, you radiate the presence of someone who sees what they want and goes after it.

Exercise: **Wanting and Relaxing Your Whole Body**

- Sit back in your chair and activate your wanting energy.

- Let it build up until you are almost shaking with the effort.

- Without letting go of the wanting to stand,

  find your feet ... hands ... head.

- Gently soften the tension in your torso.

- As you breathe, let the tension and energy of wanting flow up ... down ... out to your extremities.

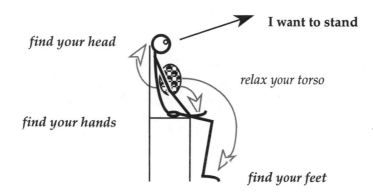

find your head **I want to stand**

relax your torso

find your hands

find your feet

Figure 11–15.

- Continue to breathe
  as you direct the energy to your whole body.

- Slowly but surely stand up.

There is no one method for "handling" life. Every encounter, even if it seems the same, is different. It is our habitual use of the same responses that make it look the same. Lasting change will remain a dream until we wake up in the midst of life's happenings and choose to act differently.

Experiment with using a different combination of feet-hands-head each time you stand. For example, emphasize legs and head on one attempt, and legs and hands on another. The more you do this you will discover that every time you want to stand, the situation is somewhat different. You are not starting in the same position each time. Your spine is not always rounded to the same degree. You are not always gazing in the same direction. You are not always in the same mood.

These observations are difficult to make when the voice of wanting is very strong. The bureaucracy of habits would prefer that you not notice differences. It uses the self-defense tactics of projecting boredom, impatience, or judgmentalness to keep you from noticing that every moment is different and you have a choice about how to respond.

The issues of waking up and choosing to act anew are found everywhere. The exercise of standing and sitting is serving as a convenient and easily observable laboratory. We recommend that you take this basic body learning into your everyday life and activities. We are sure that you will uncover many interesting and valuable experiences.

GETTING UNSTUCK FROM YOUR HABITS OF FEELING

The inherent preferences of organization are clarity, certainty and perfection. The inherent nature of human relationships involves ambiguity, uncertainty and imperfection. How one honors, balances, and integrates the needs of both is the real trick of management.

—Richard Tanner Pascale and Anthony Athos

AN ACTOR AFTER the first reading of a script will often turn to the director and ask, "What is the motivation?" The actor wants to know more about what moves this character to act and respond, the deeper drives and quirks that make this person unique. This is a request for information about the character's internal actions.

In order to step into the written character and make it live, the actor needs to know the feeling dynamics that move this fictional person to make the choices that he or she makes. The better the actor, the greater the depth of feeling that we, the audience, can perceive.

In the theater of everyday life, the task of stepping into a new way of being is just like that faced by the actor stepping into a role. The script represents your new vision or goals. Weaving together gestures, thoughts, and feelings, the character is made alive and real. The task of successfully combining our feelings with our actions is not just the task of the actor, but of anyone trying to make a lasting and authentic change.

Being able to work with feeling is one of the most important skills that an individual can possess. We have been caught in a dilemma with regards to our feelings. On one hand, we have been counseled that we must be in touch with them. Simultaneously, we are aware that the inappropriate expression of feelings can be counterproductive. This tension can be summarized this way:

**If you act out everything you feel,
you are going to get into trouble.**

**If you do not feel everything you feel,
you are going to get into even greater trouble.**

Charles Darwin, in his studies on the expression of emotion in animals and humans, noticed that every feeling state is a particular shaping of the musculature. An easily observable example is the relationship between a collapsed chest and spine and the subjective experience of depression. Posture and muscle tension play a significant role in determining what and how we feel. In spite of all the efforts we make to change our thoughts and actions, our personal bureaucracy can stay frozen in old patterns. The glue that maintains old patterns is our habits of feeling.

We have designed a series of exercises to achieve two results: they will allow you to experience for yourself the reality of Darwin's observation, and second, they will help you develop the awareness and skill to use the muscle/feeling connection in changing your life.

These exercises provide you with an alternative perspective on feelings. A new appreciation of feelings is necessary to accomplish your goals. In the following chapters you will learn to

1. experience the fact that feelings are inseparable from muscular tension patterns

2. use Centered Presence to help you see both the general and the personal ways that you are moved by specific feeling states

3. identify the typical ways you shift from "positive" to "negative" moods

4. teach you how to retool your habits of feeling by purposefully engaging them

12

TURNING YOUR NEGATIVE FEELINGS INTO GOLD

ALL OF US have grown up learning to defend ourselves against one particular feeling or another. If you look up the word *feeling* in the dictionary, you will discover a wealth of meanings

- the sense of touch
- a susceptibility to impressions
- emotion
- the background and quality of awareness
- belief
- a sympathetic aesthetic response
- passion

The human experience called feeling is not a mystery that we intend to resolve. We are more concerned with cultivating a greater skill in working with it. There are several underlying themes connecting all of these different ways of using the word *feeling*.

Feeling is a whole body response that involves our biochemistry, our psyche, and our muscles. There are two ways to approach feelings. Retooling on the Run integrates both of them.

1. **Feeling is related to movement.** We are moved toward pleasure and away from pain.

2. **Feeling is related to interpretation.** It is possible to interpret a pleasurable sensation as being dangerous. In that case, we move away from it. What is painful may be interpreted as being necessary. In that case, we move toward it.

What we are used to feeling, we call familiar and comfortable. Comfortable is the nervous system's way of saying that this state is often repeated. The feeling of comfort is one of the most powerful weapons that the bureaucracy of habits uses to defend itself against change.

Anything that is different, no matter if it is healthier, more effective, or what we really want, is the enemy of our habits. What we are *not* used to feeling, we call uncomfortable, strange, and weird. Therefore, while we are in the throes of change it is important to remember that the feeling of uncomfortableness is *only* an interpretation.

Many people are afraid to work with their feelings. They are so used to overcontrolling themselves that being moved, whether by old and unwanted feelings or by new and unfamiliar ones, seems like being out of control.

Control, as we learned it, has the side effect of suppressing movement and change. In that context, being moved portends danger. However, if you listen to the experiences of athletes, musicians, master martial artists, or creative individuals in any sphere, you come away with a very different perspective. **Letting go on purpose or choosing to be moved is considered to be at the heart of control.**

POSTURE AND FEELINGS

When uncomfortable feelings arise, your bureaucracy activates its immune-system-like defenses. Even if it is just a low-intensity experience, the defense forces act as though a total invasion and life-threatening situation is present. Once these are triggered, you are in survival mode. In this state, it is very difficult to either remember your new goals or act to achieve them.

However, if you purposefully expose yourself to low levels of uncomfortableness, then you can progressively desensitize the habit

defenses. This method corresponds to that used by physicians in the treatment of allergies. They give you small doses of the allergen in order to build up your immune system. Using the same principle, you can convince your defense system to relax and allow new and unfamiliar feelings.

In designing these experiments we used two interrelated concepts: 1. posture shapes feeling, and 2. feeling shapes posture.

Exercise: **Explore Inconsistencies between Feeling and Posture**

Figure 12–1.

- While sitting or standing, collapse your chest and spine.

- Say to yourself, *"I am happy.*
  This is the happiest day of my life."

- Now pick up your chest and smile.

- Say to yourself, *"I am depressed.*
  This is the worst day of my life."

Did you notice the strange lack of coherence or fit between your words and how you felt? Down and happy don't really make sense together. Neither does up and depressed.

See what happens if you pick up your chest and say, "I am happy." Now this is a fit. Happy and up make sense together. Similarly, down and depressed fit together.

The logic of the body is built upon correspondences such as these. At this stage of the journey, understanding why this is so is not as important as feeling *isn't it interesting* the way it fits together. This is why we say that posture and feeling are related.

STRETCHING YOUR REPERTOIRE

All feelings are important. They are voices of our organs and of our animal heritage. They are our allies in the work of accomplishment. They are also a medium for our perception of the spiritual side of life.

The next exercise explores three pairs of feeling states. The muscular practices will be followed by a commentary on some of the interesting issues that reside in these states. Our purpose is to stretch your muscles of feeling and believing. The "feelings" that we will explore in this section are: angry and peaceful, happy and anxious, frightened and open.

Exercise: Feeling Peaceful

- Imagine feeling PEACEFUL
  and let your muscles change to fit the feeling.

- Return to Centered Presence

Find ... your feet
... your hands
... your head
... your breath

How does your posture shift as you evoke "peaceful"? Do you straighten up? Do you sink down? Do you move forward or backward? Which muscles tighten and which relax?

How does your inner dialogue shift? Does it become more positive or negative? Are the "voices" louder or softer?

- Evoke "peaceful" several times with increasing intensity of feeling.

Exercise: Feeling Angry

- Imagine feeling ANGRY
  and let your muscles change to fit the feeling.

- Return to Centered Presence

Find ... your feet
... your hands
... your head
... your breath

How does your posture shift as you evoke "angry"? Do you straighten up? Do you sink down? Do you move forward or backward? Which muscles tighten and which relax?

How does your inner dialogue shift? Does it become more positive or negative? Are the "voices" louder or softer?

- Evoke "angry" several times with increasing intensity of feeling.

Christopher: Session #3

The most important lesson that Christopher learned from his previous session was that it was possible to have a controlled and partial "let go." His experiences with the practices led him to the realization that his personal ("this is the way I am") strategy was much too limiting. While it worked very well when the stress levels were low, it actually contributed to problem when the tensions grew. When he felt attacked, his objectivity and ability to analyze complex situations transformed into irritability, frustration, and anger.

Christopher was now ready to wrestle with what was going on beneath his head, not analytically (which was the comfortable way) but muscularly. The practices that he learned in the last two sessions were designed to build a foundation structure that would support the new skill that he wanted to develop. We began by using the Centered Presence exercise (*Find your feet ... hands ... head ... breath*) both to expand his perceptions and to increase his leverage for producing the appropriate muscular shifts.

Next, we led Christopher through a quick version of Pause and Let Go while standing and sitting so that he could 1. warm up his basic relaxation skills, and 2. notice which muscles repeatedly got tight and needed to be softened. Now we were ready to dive into the muscles of feeling. We asked him to recall a time when he was frustrated and angry, and to really get into the mood. Then he was asked to let go of the memory, come back to now and shake out the tension that built up. We repeated this process with different situations and people to find out if there was a pattern to his tightness. Christopher discovered that no matter what the trigger or excuse, he tightened in the same places: neck, jaw and stomach. He started to laugh as he told us of his persistent headaches and the ulcer for which he had been treated.

We were now ready for the final step. We asked him to recall one of his more difficult memories. This time we suggested that in the midst of it he relax his stomach muscles, move his jaw around, and take a breath. To his amazement he discovered that the negative and intense emotional charge that had always been connected to this memory just vanished. He tried this with several other memories and reported that the same thing happened. Not only that, he also reported that his internal conversation shifted and he saw other possibilities in each situation that he had never before noticed. We advised Christopher that unless he took the time to work with this exercise, by himself and with his imagination, that his ability to use it—when he really needed it— would fade away.

TWO POLES OF FEELING

The realm of feelings has been likened to an ocean filled with currents and waves. The dynamism of this world has given rise to the concepts of connectedness and polarity. Feelings, just like magnets, have poles. We call them positive and negative feelings. Neither one exists without the other. And feelings, just like people, live in families. No matter how far away you live from each other, and no matter what you think about each other, you still are part of a family.

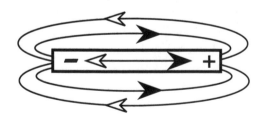

Figure 12–2.

Angry and peaceful are two members of the same family. Anger has a more contractive tone, and hence we call it negative. Peaceful has a more expansive tone and is therefore called positive. There are situations in which anger, in one form or another, is the most appropriate or best response. There are other times when being peaceful is the least appropriate or worst possible response.

When you are angry, "It matters!" When you are peaceful, "Everything's O.K." *Holding on* in order to establish control, or *letting go* of your resistance to events are intimately related. To have more of one, you have to appreciate, more deeply, the other. Each can be done poorly and each can be done well.

When you are peaceful, it is much easier to give way to the birth of a change. Peaceful done well grants you the strength and skill to recognize and resist an inappropriate or imposed change. If you imagine that the arrival of change is accompanied by a knocking at the door, then peaceful opens the door and greets the change.

When you are angry you are more likely to slam the door shut or to throw it open, prepared to do battle. There are times when this is the best move you can make, and of course there are times when this is either inappropriate or ineffective. The real issue here is whether your bureaucracy has the flexibility to choose the best response.

Since anger and peacefulness are related, you need both of them. Imagine being able to balance ease and strength, being able to grasp without crushing, to be clear and not fixated, to have delicacy of feeling, a subtler level of discernment, and to be able to move like a powered sailboat.

If you repeat the previous two exercises—Feeling Peaceful and Angry—a number of times, you may discover your historical and personal bias in the domain of feeling. You may find that the bureaucracy of your habits either does not want to let go of the anger or to have your peace disturbed. *Isn't that interesting?*

Exercise: Feeling Happy

- Imagine feeling HAPPY
  and let your muscles change to fit the feeling.

- Return to Centered Presence

Find . . . your feet
. . . your hands
. . . your head
. . . your breath

How does your posture shift as you evoke "happy"? Do you straighten up? Do you sink down? Do you move forward or backward? Which muscles tighten and which relax?

How does your inner dialogue shift? Does it become more positive or negative? Are the "voices" louder or softer?

- Evoke "happy" several times with increasing intensity of feeling.

Exercise: **Feeling Anxious**

- Imagine feeling ANXIOUS
  and let your muscles change to fit the feeling.

- Return to Centered Presence

Find . . . your feet
. . . your hands
. . . your head
. . . your breath

How does your posture shift as you evoke "anxious"? Do you straighten up? Do you sink down? Do you move forward or backward? Which muscles tighten and which relax?

How does your inner dialogue shift? Does it become more positive or negative? Are the "voices" louder or softer?

- Evoke "anxious" several times with increasing intensity of feeling.

Pauline: Session #3

It had become quite clear to Pauline that she expended a great deal of energy avoiding being "down." Even though she could see the direct benefit of "finding her feet," she reported that she either forgot to do it or she did not do it long enough so that it could work. Authentic change requires more than learning a new skill. A new future also requires a new interpretation and experience of one's past. For this session we decided to explore what happened to her when she found herself encountering "down."

We began with the *down* of "find your feet." We took her through a long and slow version of the exercise. After just a few seconds she reported that she was feeling impatient and jumpy, and she wanted the exercise to be over. As soon as we stopped, she stood up, moved around, and began to speak in an animated tone.

Next we asked her to recall a situation, past or present, in which she had to deal with lots of details. As she began to focus on all of the pieces of the project, she realized that her physical response was just the same as with finding her feet. Somehow Pauline's personal bureaucracy interpreted "down" as unsettling or even frightening. She saw that her "up" mood and high energy level was, to a large extent, a habit, a way of picking herself up to avoid being down.

Making a major behavioral shift involves facing parts of one's self that have previously been avoided. Cheng Man Ch'ing, a famous T'ai Chi master, once said, "You will be sick until you are sick of being sick." Pauline declared that she was sick of letting this "anxiety" rule her.

She was asked to purposefully evoke *down*, either by finding her feet or imagining a work situation where attention to details was required. When the anxiety energy turned on, her job was to not move, to breathe and discover that she could survive the intensity. After a few breaths, she was to gently shake the tension out of her limbs, and then go ahead to the next task.

This practice teaches the body that it can simultaneously hold intensity and release excess tension. In order to be able to access this bodily knowing when she needed it, we suggested that she practice 1. in the morning before work, 2. when she came home from work, 3. before and after important meetings.

THE MOVEMENTS OF FEELING

Feelings *are* difficult to talk about and not just because of our unique histories and education. The family that includes both happiness and anxiety has something to do with the movement of going forward and encountering a new situation.

When we are anxious we **pull back from going ahead.** This is like fear in that it has the quality of pulling back, but it differs in that the movement is an internal one. The movement of anxiety can be felt as a tensing or pulling inward of the chest, as opposed to the external act of stepping back from the encounter. This muscular tensing that we are associating with "anxiety" is not done with the large muscles of the pectorals, but with the smaller muscles of the chest wall.

When we are relaxed and our heart is not restrained, we intuitively understand that the real answers to life's questions are dynamic and multilayered. However, when the chest tightens, the integrity of our vision fragments. Anxiety seems to increase as we frantically scramble for the parts and call whatever we happen to gather up as the **answer.** This piece of the whole to which we anchor ourselves must now be protected at all costs.

When our heart is open and relaxed, when we are in the feeling state of "happiness," the voices of "I know" and "I don't know" support each other. Even in the midst of "not having a clue as to what is going on," there is the feeling of self-esteem, the voice of a knower. Even when you are positive that you are completely correct, there is the feeling of humbleness and the willingness to be wrong and to learn.

the heart is relaxed

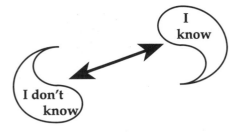

the heart is tense

Figure 12–3.

But when the tension mounts, the flow between knowing and not knowing grows turbulent and difficult to cross. Once this happens there is a real shift in how we perceive and evaluate what is going on. Uncertainty seems to take on more importance. The voice of "I do not know and I am hesitant to risk" grows stronger and threatens to overpower our ability to go ahead into the unknown.

When you are happy, the path of least resistance is to move into going ahead. The chest expands as if to meet whatever adventure is to come. In this space of feeling, uncertainty and not knowing are not a problem. This is not easy to do. To maintain happiness or lightness of being in the midst of the difficulties of life requires a special strength.

The strength to be happy, despite the circumstances, is developed through practice. For example, in addition to the traditional methods of reminding yourself of the beauty of life and how much you have to be thankful for, we recommend a few simple muscular maneuvers.

To begin, imagine being happy and notice if your muscles shift in response to the feeling possibility. In particular, notice if your chest "is willing" to lift up and expand outward.

Observe yourself over a period of time to ascertain if you have the postural habit of holding your chest down and pulled in. This is not a negative trait. There are many emotions that require this chest posture in order to reveal themselves. In particular, the feeling state of being grounded cannot easily operate when the chest is held up too high.

If you discover that your chest "likes to stay down," then we suggest that you practice lifting it up. Do not attempt this by directly picking up your chest. When we directly counter a bureaucratic habit, it is like waving a red flag in front of a bull; it is an invitation to fight.

Instead, begin breathing up into your chest. Start with a small inhale. Notice if the breath rushes up into your face. If so, place your hands on your chest, and use your inhale to push into your hands. This will indirectly lift up your chest. The next step, once you link inhaling with the chest rising, is to allow your facial muscles to lift.

The timing is: 1. inhale, 2. chest lifts, 3. face lifts. Happiness cannot easily show itself when the face cannot smile. When you have the choice about whether your face can smile then you can choose to keep the smile to yourself. Until then, you might be withholding happiness from everyone, especially yourself.

Happiness is often misunderstood. Many people believe that if they had no anxiety or fear they would be happy. Happy and anxious are members of the same family. You cannot have one without the other. Going forward without any possibility of openness to pulling back can be characterized as acting like a Pollyanna or simply having suicidal trust.

The real issue is not whether or not you pull back. It is whether you are stuck in the habit of either pulling back or going forward without any choice of acting differently.

In the martial arts, the ability to move into any situation with a positive attitude while at the same time examining the situation for potential dangers is called **karate spirit.** With this strength of feeling, you can expand your heart even in the midst of danger or disappointment.

If you repeat the previous two exercises—Feeling Happy and Anxious—a number of times, you may discover your historical and personal bias in the domain of feeling. You may find that the bureaucracy of your habits either does not want to let go of the anxiety or is uneasy with happiness. *Isn't that interesting?*

Exercise: Feeling Open

- Imagine feeling OPEN
  and let your muscles change to fit the feeling.

- Return to Centered Presence

Find . . . your feet
. . . your hands
. . . your head
. . . your breath

How does your posture shift as you evoke "open"? Do you straighten up? Do you sink down? Do you move forward or backward? Which muscles tighten and which relax?

How does your inner dialogue shift? Does it become more positive or negative? Are the "voices" louder or softer?

- Evoke "open" several times with increasing intensity of feeling.

Exercise: **Feeling Frightened**

- Imagine feeling FRIGHTENED
  and let your muscles change to fit the feeling.

- Return to Centered Presence

Find . . . your feet
. . . your hands
. . . your head
. . . your breath

How does your posture shift as you evoke "frightened"? Do you straighten up? Do you sink down? Do you move forward or backward? Which muscles lighten and which relax?

How does your inner dialogue shift? Does it become more positive or negative? Are the "voices" louder or softer?

- Evoke "frightened" several times with increasing intensity of feeling.

DANGER MIND

Fear cuts to the core. The rush of adrenaline that accompanies it mobilizes your whole body for action. It is as though your biochemistry is asking, "Should I back away from the touch of the approaching encounter? Or should I let it touch me and then move me?" Fear and openness are two members of a very important family that also includes vulnerability, adaptability, resiliency, responsiveness, and the ability to draw from the wellspring of life and wisdom.

The habit of fear is very debilitating. Many methods are offered to help you change it. "Push through your fear," "There is nothing to fear," and "Bury your fears" are three popular approaches. The abilities of pushing through, rising above, and holding down are important for your success, yet there is still something missing. The secret ingredient is, of course, acceptance. But what does this mean and how do you do it?

The warrior master is often used as an image of fearlessness. Such people are viewed as being beyond fear. This is not the case at all. There is a very large difference between being unafraid to be afraid and having no fear at all. If you could eliminate fear from your life, you would also be shutting off one source of your vitality and intuition.

Adrenaline speeds us up. The mind moves at hyperspeed trying to figure out the situation. To do this, our scanning intelligence has to lift itself up to get a better view. If there is nothing to be seen, the natural animal relaxes back into the "body," shakes off the adrenaline rush, and goes about its business. However, with the habit of fear, we forget to relax back down.

The natural mind lives in harmony with the flow of life. The wariness and tension of the "danger mind" disturbs the flow. In order to be sure, we need to check and double check our perceptions. In order to be sure, we have to stop the flow and hold everything very still so we can see with certainty what is going on. Continually searching for danger, we internally overprocess our feelings, squeezing out the water or the feeling of the feeling, and instead, we hold on to our thoughts about our feelings.

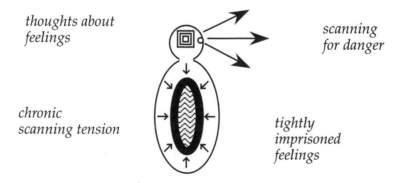

thoughts about feelings

scanning for danger

chronic scanning tension

tightly imprisoned feelings

Figure 12–4.

Fear and defensiveness go hand in hand. From their point of view, the possibility of openness feels like having no defenses and being incapable of stopping someone from hurting or violating you. To be vulnerable or open is to be exposed. You can be touched and hence be wounded. When vulnerability is perceived as a liability, it is hard to imagine being both open and powerful.

This is the view of danger mind, not of the natural mind. Openness is about having the possibility of being touched and moved and having choice in how you defend yourself. Feeling like your boundaries are "frozen" in an open position or being in a condition of such paralysis that you cannot "close the doors" is defenselessness, not openness.

The habit of pseudovulnerability strongly challenges your self-esteem and confidence. It is the product of an internal action of pulling away from the possible contact. If, when someone came toward you, you pulled your chest inward and downward until your back rounded, just slightly, and you did not move your feet, then you would be in the muscular shape of feeling unprotected and easily hurt.

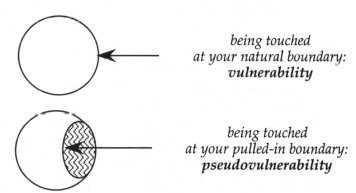

*being touched
at your natural boundary:*
vulnerability

*being touched
at your pulled-in boundary:*
pseudovulnerability

Figure 12–5.

The logic of fear is the black and white of either/or distinctions. Either I am protected, or I am defenseless. The logic of openness is flowing, dynamic, and filled with shades of gray. In the feeling state of openness, I feel secure in my ability to defend myself. I know that I can tighten up in an instant, if necessary. I know that my integrity and dignity are so deeply embedded that I will not be destroyed by our contact.

Dorothy: Session #3

Dorothy began with a series of questions that had been bothering her all month. Why didn't she use her new skills when she really needed them? Why did certain kinds of interactions trigger superdrive and not others? Why was she so leery of "opening up" in the midst of conflict? What was she afraid of? As she put it, "Tell me what I need to know to handle this issue, once and for all. Give me a target and I'll go for it."

One of Dorothy's greatest fears was that if she were to show her caring side, she would lose her driving force, her competitive edge. We reassured her that she was right, this was a legitimate issue. Most of us move through life ruled by what we like to call danger mind. When it is in charge, we see our choices as black or white. The larger field of options and choices vanishes and our boundaries tighten in self-protectiveness. Dorothy was asking if it was possible to break out of this either/or box and bring together these two crucial parts of herself. Rather than being either caring or powerful, she wanted to be both.

Through this discussion, Dorothy saw that one of the ways she could tell if she was acting from danger mind was to say to herself, "*I am powerful and caring.*" If her natural mind were in control, she would "hear" murmurs of agreement and offers of constructive criticism. However, if danger mind was in charge, the "voices" would be negative, the criticism self-negating, and the options very limited.

If she found herself in the danger zone, she was to *find her feet*, relax, and take a fresh breath. Then *find her head,* look around to see if the situation was precarious or safe, and take a fresh breath. Next, *find her hands*, breathe into her chest, smile, and say "*I am powerful and caring.*" The game was to practice until she believed with her whole body that she could be both. She knew that this would not be easy and would require a new, positive use of her superdrive.

STAYING OPEN IN THE MIDST OF FEAR

After many years of practicing to relax in the midst of combat, martial artists come to the realization that danger mind, while more impulsive, is actually slower than the natural mind of openness. All those thoughts of worry, expectation, and strategy clog up the pathways of action and perception. Your ideas about the attacker can get in your way of seeing what is actually going on.

Even more important, especially regarding the issue of relationship, is the distancing that chronic fear produces. In the feeling state of pseudovulnerability, the path of least resistance is to not let the other person get too close. This can lead to the habit of loneliness with its consequences of, "I don't need anyone" or "I am needy for connection."

The energy you use to control your fears takes away from the energy you can use to express yourself. To push an unwanted feeling, such as fear, away from consciousness, you have to tighten and hold whole groups of muscles. These same muscles could be involved, in a different way, in the act of expressing your intent or desire.

The "family of feelings" concept teaches that even if you do not like a particular quality or state or part of yourself, you should not attempt to close it off. Whenever a strong wall is placed between feelings or people, love cannot flow. To pull away from being hurt only makes the hurting grow. If you can stay with the feelings or the contact, you are in a much better position to both discover what is really going on, and to do something about it. This is the power of vulnerability and openness.

If you repeat the previous two exercises—Feeling Open and Frightened—a number of times, you may discover your historical and personal bias in the domain of feeling. You may find that the bureaucracy of your habits either does not want to let go of the fear or is uncomfortable with openness. *Isn't that interesting?*

13

CONSCIOUSLY CHANGING THE ROLLERCOASTER OF FEELING

AT THE HEART of it, we all share the same ocean of feeling. We all have access to the full human range of expression and experience. In this primordial state, feelings are free to shift and change as the situation or one's "state of mind" shifts and changes.

From the perspective of the learned or historical self, we each live in our own artificial ocean. For each of us the currents and weather patterns move differently. To the degree that our animal nature is neither recognized nor appreciated, the individual experiences himself or herself alone.

Creating new habits of feeling has never been easy, because the bureaucratic defense forces battle fiercely against change. Sun Tzu, the famous Chinese general, believed that winning is best enjoyed when it occurs without any unnecessary fighting. The secret to such a victory lies, he said, "in knowing both your enemy and your self." Your primary enemy is your lack of awareness of your habits.

The first phase of the process of retooling your habits of feeling requires a bit of simple detective work on your part. Before we can begin the job of subverting the dominant paradigm, we have to know what it is.

Exercise: Identifying the Pattern of our Habits of Feeling

Step 1: Contemplate and then write answers to the following questions.

- *What are the signs by which you know that you are in a **positive mood**?*

    1. What do you feel in this state?

    2. What you think in this mood?

    3. How do you typically move?

    4. How do you react to people and situations?

    5. How does the future and/or past look to you from here?

- *What are the signs by which you know that you are in a **negative mood**?*

    1. What do you feel in this state?

    2. What you think in this mood?

    3. How do you typically move?

    4. How do you react to people and situations?

    5. How does the future and/or past look to you from here?

- *What are the signs you are **losing the positive mood?***

    1. What do you feel in this state?

    2. What you think in this mood?

    3. How do you typically move?

    4. How do you react to people and situations?

    5. How does the future and/or past look to you from here?

- *What are the signs you are **leaving the negative mood?***

    1. What do you feel in this state?

    2. What you think in this mood?

    3. How do you typically move?

    4. How do you react to people and situations?

    5. How does the future and/or past look to you from here?

Step 2: Create a summary by reading over each of the four lists and choosing several key words from each.

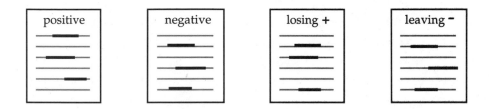

Figure 13–1.

Step 3: Create a map of your habits of feeling by writing these words in the appropriate spaces in the following diagram, or draw your own on a fresh piece of paper.

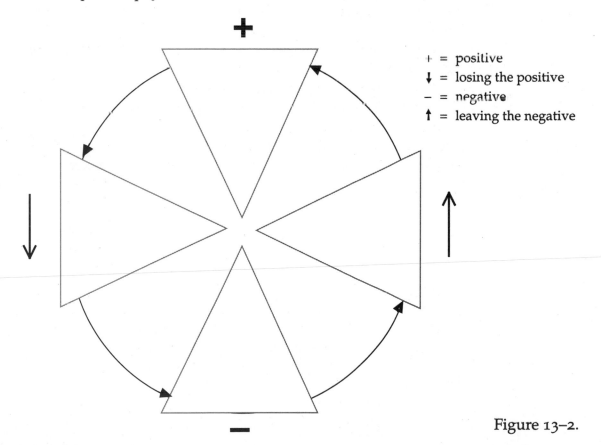

Figure 13–2.

PHASE 1: DOING THE PATTERN ON PURPOSE

Change is an uphill battle until we can neutralize the automatic defenses of our personal bureaucracy. Once these are relaxed, the whole system is more amenable for discussions about change. Our job is to convince our bureaucracy that the actions we want to take are not a danger to its status quo.

The method is to do on purpose the same actions that the bureaucracy does automatically. Since we are asking it to do what it already does, it has no reason to fight. But we are doing this without the habitual triggers, both situational and internal. This generates a gentle and pervasive perturbation rather than the more disruptive upsets that it knows how to fight. This will gently begin to unravel some of the cobwebs and soften some of the glue that holds everything too tightly in place.

Bureaucratic defenses work very much like an immune system. Their most important actions are to decide what belongs and what doesn't. **By interfering with the defenses, just below their threshold for aggressive reaction, you can evoke an internal housecleaninglike series of actions.** The bureaucracy of your own nervous system now becomes interested in the same questions that interest you. *What do I have to let go of? What do I have to keep? What do I need to add on?*

OPENING THE BUREAUCRACY

*shifting from
positive to negative*

Figure 13–3.

Exercise: Shifting from Positive to Negative Moods

Step 1: Activate the Positive

- Read over the key words that you wrote for the **positive** mood.

- As you read the words, remember the **experiences** that fit them.

- As your state of mind begins to shift, encourage your **muscles** to also shift.

- Let your **posture** also begin to shift.

- Begin to notice how your internal dialogue or **thinking** process shifts to fit the new muscular balance.

- **Move** around the room in this whole body state.
  How does life look to you in this state?
  What do you want to do?
  How would you react to obstacles or difficulties?

Step 2: Activate the Negative

- Read over the key words that you wrote for the **negative** mood.

- As you read the words, remember the **experiences** that fit them.

- As your state of mind begins to shift, encourage your **muscles** to also shift.

- Let your **posture** also begin to shift.

- Begin to notice how your internal dialogue or **thinking** process shifts to fit the new muscular balance.

- **Move** around the room in this whole body state.
  How does life look to you in this state?
  What do you want to do?
  How would you react to obstacles or difficulties?

Step 3: Generate a Flow

- Activate the **positive** mood,
  with its associated muscles, posture, experience, and
  thoughts.

- Let your attention shift and activate the **negative** mood,
  with its associated muscles, posture, experience and
  thoughts

- Reactivate the **positive** phase.
  Let the "energies" grow.

- Reactivate the **negative** phase.
  Let the "energies" grow.

- Continue to **shift back and forth** between the positive and
  the negative.

- When you choose to stop, pause for a moment and listen
  for what your whole body can tell you.

- Return to Centered Presence

Anthony: Session #3

In his work to date, Anthony had practiced exercises of **intent,** which taught him that he could "be in charge," and exercises of **intensity,** which proved that he could hold his ground even in situations of conflict. He reported that he enjoyed using these new abilities, but at the same time they felt uncomfortable and inauthentic. As he put it, it didn't feel natural.

What Anthony really meant was that it didn't feel **normal.** Whatever we are used to doing feels comfortable, natural, and right. This is how bureaucracies work. This is how they defend against change. The pull toward the comfortable is a very powerfully seductive force. If we can accept that this pull is real, then we can more easily recognize when it is working on us and more skillfully work with it to bring forth our new normal.

For the first step we asked Anthony to map out his normal cycle of feelings using the questions: What are the signs that you are in a "positive" or a "negative" mood? What happens to your self-confidence in each? How do you react to stress or conflict? What possibilities do you envision? Next we took Anthony through his personal cycle several times, until he could feel his posture shifting with each mood. These muscular keys were then added to his map. Finally, we led him through the cycle again but this time using the postures. Instead of asking him to feel "happy and confident," the words he wrote in his map, we asked him to lift his chest and smile. Instead of "depressed and directionless," he was to collapse his chest and relax his jaw.

By traveling through his normal cycle of feelings, but using a brand new approach (postures lead feelings), Anthony was undermining his habits' defenses and opening the door to deep and authentic change. To speed the process along, we added the following touch. Before leaving the negative mood, he was to use the Centered Presence exercise (*Find your feet … hands … head … breath*).

RESISTING THE NATURAL FLOW OF FEELINGS

Now that we have engaged the bureaucracy's attention, let's open it up some more. Bureaucracies are by nature conservative. They like to hold on to what they have. The difficulties emerge when we try to hold onto something that inherently changes.

There is a story about an English king who attempted to apply his divine right prerogative to the ocean tides. No matter what he said or did, nature did not respond to his commands. Some life processes are too powerful to be directly controlled. Our feeling nature is like the ocean. It has currents and tides.

If you do not feel everything you feel, you are going to get into trouble. Whether you like it or not, your positive moods are connected to your negative moods. Most probably you prefer the positive to the negative. That's the problem. The desire to hold on to the positive feeling state and get rid of or ignore the negative feeling state often leads to

- excess tension and stress

- the crash-and-burn syndrome

- a deep valley of depression and struggle

- the "need" for more seminars

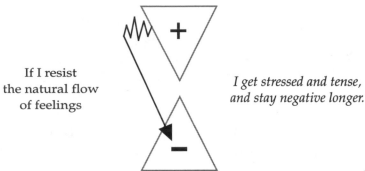

If I resist
the natural flow
of feelings

*I get stressed and tense,
and stay negative longer.*

Figure 13–4.

By fighting the natural flow of feelings we play into the hands of habit's defenses. However, if we work with the natural flow, we can begin to shift the game to produce the conditions that allow our desires for change to grow and flourish.

PHASE 2: DOING THE PATTERN ON PURPOSE

Any pattern of activity that repeats itself takes on the qualities of solidity and consistency. This pattern is experienced as familiar and feels comfortable. It feels like, "This is me. This is the way the world is for me." This sense of normality and comfort is both a gift and a liability. It is a gift in the sense that it allows you to relax the conscious effort necessary to monitor and direct your daily activities. It is a liability in that it brings a decreased awareness of yourself-in-action.

Reprogramming a bureaucracy is like going under the hood of a car. The greatest leverage for real change comes from working directly with the mechanisms that underlie and support your habits and their associated experiences and actions. We will now slow down the process of shifting from positive to negative in order to reveal the intermediary stage that lies between them.

OPENING THE BUREAUCRACY

cycling through your habits

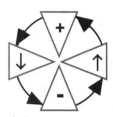

Figure 13-5.

Exercise: Traveling the Whole Mood Cycle

Step 1: Activate the Positive

- Activate the **positive** mood,
  with its associated muscles, posture, experience and thoughts.

- **Notice** the shifts in your internal dialogue or **thinking** process.

- **Move** around the room in this whole body state.
  How does life look to you in this state?
  What do you want to do?
  How would you react to obstacles or difficulties?

Step 2: Activate the Losing the Positive

- Read over the key words for the **losing the positive** mood.

- As you read the words, remember the **experiences** that fit them.

- As your state of mind begins to shift,
  encourage your **muscles** to also shift.

- Let your **posture** also begin to shift.

- Notice the shifts in your internal dialogue or **thinking** process.

- **Move** around the room in this whole body state.
  How does life look to you in this state?
  What do you want to do?
  How would you react to obstacles or difficulties?

Step 3: Activate the Negative

- Activate the **negative** mood, with its associated muscles, posture, experience and thoughts.

- **Notice** the shifts in your internal dialogue or **thinking** process.

- **Move** around the room in this whole body state.
  How does life look to you in this state?
  What do you want to do?
  How would you react to obstacles or difficulties?

Step 4: Activate the Leaving the Negative

- Read over the key words for the **leaving the negative** mood.

- As you read the words, remember the **experiences** that fit them.

- As your state of mind begins to shift, encourage your **muscles** to also shift.

- Let your **posture** also begin to shift.

- Notice the shifts in your internal dialogue or **thinking** process.

- **Move** around the room in this whole body state.
  How does life look to you in this state?
  What do you want to do?
  How would you react to obstacles or difficulties?

Step 5: Generate a Flow

- Go through the cycle several times.

- At each phase, linger long enough for the "energies" to grow.

- When you choose to stop, pause for a moment and listen for what your whole body can tell you.

- Return to Centered Presence

PHASE 3: RETOOLING THE MOOD CYCLE

You have been accumulating a special kind of knowledge about yourself. It combines thinking and feeling with sensing. In other words, by these simple activities, you have been cultivating Centered Presence. Paying attention to your thinking or inner dialogue is another way to *find your head*. Paying attention to what you are feeling is another way to *find your hands*. Paying attention to your muscles and posture is another way to *find your feet*. Moving through the whole habit cycle is another way to *find the breath*.

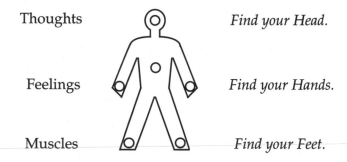

Thoughts — *Find your Head.*

Feelings — *Find your Hands.*

Muscles — *Find your Feet.*

Figure 13–6.

When we first presented Centered Presence, we used it to defuse the intensity of an angry feeling state. Now let's use it to begin the process of retooling your habits of feeling. Through practice, you can transform your experience from being predictable into being a spontaneous flow, filled with creative possibilities.

Exercise: Retooling the Mood Cycle

Step 1: Retooling the Negative

- Use your key words to shift to the **negative** feeling state.

- Let every muscle in your body shift to fit the mood.

- Let your thoughts and feelings also shift to fit the mood.

- Let the energy of this state grow.

- Return to Centered Presence.

**Find . . . your feet
. . . your hands
. . . your head
. . . your breath**

- Let your muscles, thoughts and feelings shift to fit Centered Presence.

- Take a fresh breath.

Step 2: Retooling Leaving the Negative

- Use your key words to shift to the **leaving the negative** feeling state.

- Let every muscle in your body shift to fit the mood.

- Let your thoughts and feelings also shift to fit the mood.

- Let the energy of this state grow.

- Return to Centered Presence.

**Find . . . your feet
. . . your hands
. . . your head
. . . your breath**

- Let your muscles, thoughts and feelings shift to fit Centered Presence.

- Take a fresh breath.

Step 3: Retooling the Positive

- Use your key words to shift to the **positive** feeling state.

- Let every muscle in your body shift to fit the mood.

- Let your thoughts and feelings also shift to fit the mood.

- Let the energy of this state grow.

- Return to Centered Presence.

 **Find . . . your feet**
. . . your hands
. . . your head
. . . your breath

- Let your muscles, thoughts and feelings shift to fit Centered Presence.

- Take a fresh breath.

Step 4: Retooling Losing the Positive

- Use your key words to shift to the **losing the positive** feeling state.

- Let every muscle in your body shift to fit the mood.

- Let your thoughts and feelings also shift to fit the mood.

- Let the energy of this state grow.

- Return to Centered Presence.

 **Find . . . your feet**
. . . your hands
. . . your head
. . . your breath

- Let your muscles, thoughts and feelings shift to fit Centered Presence.

- Take a fresh breath.

Step 5: Building New Habits

- Repeat the cycle several times.

- Practice recapturing Centered Presence in the midst of a familiar negative experience.

You probably noticed that returning to Centered Presence in the midst of a habitual mood shifted your experience. People who have regularly practiced Centered Presence report that it seems to take the bite out of the negative while it deepens the positive.

Figure 13–7.

The next move is up to you. Sometime in the near future you will find yourself "attacked" by your habits. Your enemy can appear in the form of a mood of negativity that throws you off balance. What are you going to do?

The easy act is to do nothing and let the game play itself out like it always does. The difficult act is to remember your ability to return to Centered Presence and to activate it while in the negative phase.

**By turning the cycle of feelings into a regular practice,
you will gain the skill and the power
to radically shift your responses to emotional situations.**

SECTION V

STALKING VERSATILITY

MOST PEOPLE PREFER to find work that is comfortable for their operating style. With change continuing to accelerate, we are called upon to step up to new and different circumstances. We are asked to go beyond our familiar styles and abilities to become more versatile. Training for versatility is different than working to learn a new behavior.

**The conscious practice of shifting from one style to another
by passing through Centered Presence
naturally produces versatility.**

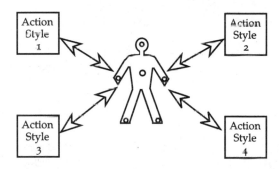

Figure V–1.

Returning to the open learning state is necessary in order to both release our prior habits and to add on or learn new action habits. This cultivates versatility in a form that is sustainable and authentic.

To train for versatility, we need a map of the territory. There are many models and typologies that label the various components of human nature.[1] These maps attempt to identify what is unique and what is universal in our behavior. Maps have two purposes: 1. to divide the world in a way that makes sense and is useful, and 2. to show you the relationship between where you are now and where you might go. Most models suggest that there is value in actively cultivating one's less familiar or underdeveloped qualities.

This section addresses the practical issues of expanding our repertoire for greater versatility, by working with the whole body underpinnings of behavior, type, and style. In particular, we are focusing on the issue of encounter, since at its core, an action style is a way of responding to encounters. **Versatility is the ability to respond appropriately as the situation warrants.**

THE ENCOUNTER WITH CHANGE

Change is an encounter with the unknown. The way you respond to the possibility of change is shaped by your historical patterns of responding to other types of encounters. Life is filled with encounters. Whether it is with people, events, or things, each encounter presents you with the possibility that you will have to change.

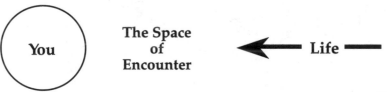

Figure V–2.

To succeed in the task of changing, you need to develop an embodied understanding of what happens in the act of encountering. You especially need to know how you historically respond, because you bring these habits to every encounter. We usually recognize these habits by the familiar thoughts and feelings that accompany them. However, at a very basic level our responses are movements in relationship to boundaries.

This next few chapters focus on the movements and postural dynamics that sustain of our habits of encounter and personal style. This series of experiments provides

1. an introduction to boundaries, stress responses, and the four primal encounter styles

2. an embodied experience of the different styles

3. a practical method for learning the encounter styles using breath, stance, and movement

4. simple practices to translate this into your everyday life

PRACTICING INTENTIONAL VERSATILITY

All contact takes place on the boundary.
—Frederick Perls, *Gestalt Therapy*

LIKE THE SPATIAL equivalent of a verbal definition, a boundary marks the territory. It separates one organism, person, or organization from another. This distinctiveness is not total, however. For just like the biological membrane of a cell, our personal boundary is semipermeable.

Cell Membrane   Personal Boundary

Figure 14–1.

A boundary is a dynamic event. It is the organ of relationship between you and the world. It belongs to both. A small change in your understanding of its role and how you use it can produce very large changes in how you respond to the world and how the world responds to you.

The "holes" in the boundary can be viewed as doors that can open and close. This rhythmic logic is found over and over again, from the beating of your heart to the inhale and exhale cycle of your lungs. When the organism encounters danger, the doors close and it is as though a shield is activated. The impulse from the outside bounces off your solid strength.

However, if this becomes a habit, then this same strength and solidness can become a barrier for your own impulses. There is a side effect to living as though the world is always dangerous. The more you need to protect yourself, the more difficult it is to express yourself.

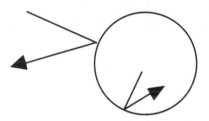

When the shield is activated, what is outside stays outside and what is within stays within.

Figure 14–2.

This condition is another example of the habit defenses in action. It is a reminder of how "fear" tends to shrink our logical capacities to a primitive either/or mode of thinking. When this occurs, our internal dialogue sounds like, *"I have to protect myself. If I don't, I'm going to get hurt. Safety means being strong and solid. Danger lies in being vulnerable. Therefore, I am going to close off any possible opening for fear of being defenseless."*

When fear rules, the dynamic nature of polarities gets covered up by the intensity of contradictions. It is very easy to fall into the pseudopolarity of protected versus defenseless.

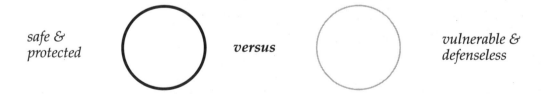

safe & protected   *versus*   vulnerable & defenseless

Figure 14–3.

In the context of this belief, being safe and protected looks like a completely enclosed boundary. If this is so, then it makes sense that being vulnerable and defenseless seems like having no boundary at all.

But what if this is not so? Warriors assert the secret to being invulnerable and unconquerable is to stay relaxed and open in the midst of the stress of the encounter. This is often called going with the flow.

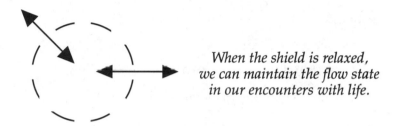

When the shield is relaxed, we can maintain the flow state in our encounters with life.

Figure 14–4.

Even for those who trust in life, there are times when you feel or even are "under attack." The natural response is to close the doors at the point of attack and stay open everywhere else. If the point of contact shifts, then you also shift where you are tensing and where you relaxing. Life is dynamic, therefore your responses to its changes must be as well.

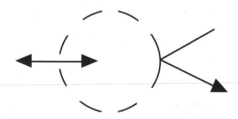

Figure 14–5.

THE STRESS AND STARTLE RESPONSES

When an animal senses the approach of danger, a deeply embedded biological action called the startle reflex is engaged. The breath stops, the limbs and the gut tighten, and the eyes and ears scan the environment. If the animal decides that it is still safe, it releases this response and returns to its relaxed, natural state.

The human animal has a startle reflex as well. However, we are not as good at releasing it and returning to a relaxed state. Have you ever noticed that

- your head, neck, and shoulders are tight?

- your breath is not as free as it "should be"?

- your joints are not flexible?

- you are continually scanning the world around you?

- you are stuck in listening to internal conversations?

These are signs that you are *stuck in startle*. Humans are more prone to this than any other animal. It may have something to do with our greater capacity for self-reflection, but whatever the cause, the effects are widespread.

When you are muscularly tight and mentally paranoid, how smoothly do you interact with others? It is difficult to be really open to differences of opinion and style while you are in the biological state of "danger mind." This is a problem for individuals, corporations, and nations alike.

When you are stuck in startle, your capacities for creativity and responsiveness are constrained. Automatic behavior is the norm. Your reactivity triggers those around you, which in turn pushes your stress buttons even further. As long as these old reactions are running the show, there is no real opportunity to do something different or new. In the heat of this everyday battle, the energy that would take your vision and transform it into an actuality is dissipated.

If you could wake up in the midst of this drama, you could shift the process. An action that has been tempered in the fire of conscious attention has a deep impact, and is not so easily forgotten. The practice of Centered Presence can help anchor you in this place of awareness and choice. As your whole body returns to your field of attention, you begin to spontaneously release both the tensions of startle and habit. This allows your perceptions to open up. Once again clear and

calm, you can see what is happening around you. The actions that follow are now more likely to produce the effects you desire.

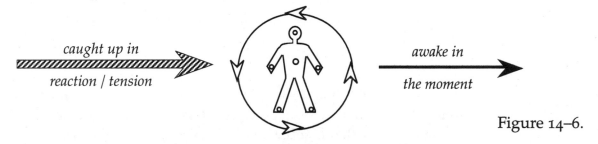

caught up in

reaction / tension

awake in

the moment

Figure 14–6.

Returning to the animal encounter with danger, the initial reflex of
startle is followed by one of four basic responses: *fight, flight, freeze,* or
faint. If the potential danger comes close, the startled animal reacts in
one of these four ways. When it feels safe again, the animal relaxes,
releasing both the tensions of its specific stress response and the general tension of the startle reflex. The cycle of animal responsiveness can
be simplified as

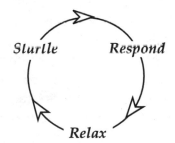

Startle   *Respond*

Relax

Figure 14–7.

With our special skills at learning and language, the human animal
complicates this rhythm remarkably. Not only have we learned to forget
to let go of startle, but we have gotten so caught up in our reactions to
our reactions and our stories about our stories that we have no idea where
the natural state even lives. Without that, there is no room for change.

THE FIVE RINGS

Throughout history people have used images drawn from nature to
talk about and make sense of the world. The hot brightness of fire

became a symbol for the creative spark that can ignite and inspire the spirit. The formlessness of water, which takes on the shape of the container, the ungraspable movement of the wind, and the solidity of the earth were also used as elements in a primordial language.

While this may sound strange to our modern Western mind, we can still find traces of this way of making distinctions in the modern scientific model of the four fundamental forces: electromagnetic, gravitational, and strong and weak nuclear. We also discover it in Jung's fourfold model of psychological types: thinking, feeling, intuition, and sensation, and in the organizational psychology models of Social Styles[1]: Analytic, Amiable, Expressive, and Driver.

To assist you in your exploration of styles of encounter, we will be using a map called the Five Rings. With it, you can harness your whole body perception and make purposeful shifts in the internal actions that sustain your habits. You will learn to do this in such a way that you will be able to transfer this movement study into your daily activities.

The best known model of this elemental language is found in the writings of Miyamoto Musashi, a sixteenth-century warrior. *A Book of Five Rings: A Guide to Strategy* has been an international classic for centuries and is now being read by a modern Western audience. Drawing upon his experience in personal combat, he declared that predictability made one unnecessarily vulnerable to one's opponents. Real power was cultivated by mastering all of the strategies. He believed that if you had access to each of them, you would become spontaneously creative and unpredictable. He called these strategies: *GROUND, WATER, FIRE, WIND,* and *VOID (SPACE).*

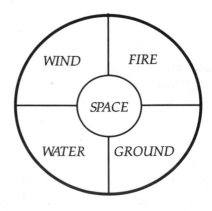

Figure 14–8.

For Musashi, the essence of the Five Rings was to be found everywhere in nature. That means that you, the reader, *already* know these strategies, albeit not by these "exotic" labels.

Exercise: **Recognizing your Response to Encounters**

- Imagine that someone you do not know is approaching.

- Imagine that they are entering the outer boundaries of your personal territory.

- Feel the pressure, stress, or tension rising as they move closer.

- Imagine that they are coming closer still, and are passing through even more personal boundaries.

- Feel the pressure, stress, or tension rising as they move closer.

  What is your response to this encounter?

  What is occurring "within" you as this person comes closer?

We are used to answering questions like this by speaking about our emotional reactions, our inner conversations, the bodily tensions we feel, and/or the historical results of such encounters. To make the type of changes in which you are interested, these awarenesses are not sufficient. You also need to know how you moved and/or wanted to move as they came closer.

Your habits, like everything else in nature, are rooted in movement. Albert Einstein echoed the Chinese masters of old when he said, "Nothing happens until something moves." The nice thing about movement is that even though it runs deep, it is accessible right where you are now. The Five Rings is a language of movement. Using it, you can reach through your stories about your responses to touch their essence.

Each of the moves represented in the Five Rings matrix below is, in itself, positive. There are times when it is appropriate to **move into** an encounter and there are times when it is appropriate to **move away** from it. There are times when you should **refuse to be moved,** and there are times when you need to allow yourself to **be moved.**

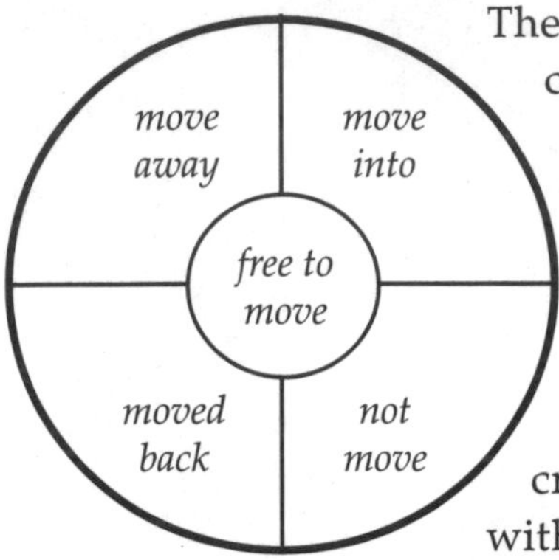

The Fifth Ring **(free to move)** represents the state where you can naturally access any and all of the four moves. From the perspective of your habits, there is no Fifth Ring. **The Fifth Ring, free to move, is about having the possibility of real choice or Intentional Versatility.** Your capacity to access its power grows as your skill at using the other Rings develops.

The bureaucracy of the nervous system is not the seat of creative thinking. It is the organ of repetition. When faced with a new problem, it only knows to use the old answers. If moving into an encounter worked once, it should always work. Therefore, whenever possible, you should act in this way over and over until it finally works. "If at first you don't succeed, try, try again."

Imagine that you want to shift from fighting all of the time to being more cooperative. Even though your "conscious" self is in alignment with this goal, and you can see the costs of remaining the way you have been, you still get caught up in conflict.

Figure 14–9.

Your daily actions and reactions are influenced by the historical layers of repetition that form the bureaucracy of your nervous system.

Figure 14–10.

Which move(s) do you use when life is going smoothly?

When you encounter difficulties?

When you do not like, understand, or value something?

FEELING WHAT YOU SEE

Movement is not limited to "body" or to words. It can also be seen and felt through visual images. Visceral reactions are very important. Your "gut" can speak to you about matters of which your head knows not.

In the following section, you will be asked to imagine four encounters, each representing a different movement response. Using imagination, you can evoke the same responses that would occur in real life. In the following images of the Five Rings, the circles represent people and the arrows are indicators of movement and direction.

Exercise: **Noticing Your Visceral Reaction to Visual Images**

Notice your visceral reactions to the interplay of circles, arrows, and words. Remember to pay attention to these bodily cues, especially when you find yourself in the midst of an intense encounter. The more you listen to your "body," the more it will speak to you.

Image #1

I am not moved by the encounter.

Figure 14–11.

You approach. I don't move.
The closer you come,
the more my walls grow solid and heavy.
You touch me. I am unmoved.

What do you viscerally feel as you look at this image from the Ring of GROUND?

Image #2

I am moved by the encounter.

Figure 14–12.

You approach. I step back.
You continue coming forward. I continue stepping back.
You stop. I stop.

You step back and move away from me.
I move forward, step by step, and return to where I started.

What do you viscerally feel as you look at this image from the Ring of WATER?

Image #3

I move into the encounter.

Figure 14–13.

You approach. I step forward to meet you.
You stop. I pause, ready to move forward again.
The encounter breeds energy and excitement.

What do you viscerally feel as you look at this image from the Ring of FIRE?

Image #4

I move away from the encounter.

Figure 14–4.

You approach. Sensing you at a distance,
I begin to pull away.
As you move forward, I step away from your touch.
The more you try to touch me, the more elusive I become.

*What do you viscerally feel as you look at this image from the
Ring of WIND?*

FOUR SCENARIOS

Let us briefly look at what might occur when two individuals with different styles interact. In Scenario #1, we examine what happens when someone with a *FIRE/GROUND* orientation meets someone with a *WATER/WIND* orientation. Viewed from the perspective of a disagreement, they have very different ways of speaking about each other.

Scenario #1:

PERSON 1 typically uses *moving into* and *not moving.*

PERSON 2 typically uses *moving back* and *moving away.*

PERSON 1   (FIRE/GROUND)   says of 2   "He's too wishy-washy."

PERSON 2   (WATER/WIND)   says of 1   "She's too aggressive."

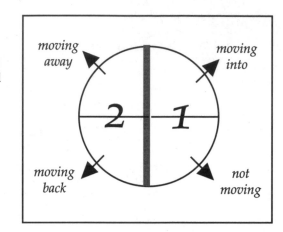

- doesn't fight
- stays relaxed

———————

- relates to
  people
- likes to
  cooperate

- pushes forward
- is focused

———————

- stands firm
- carries through

Figure 14–15.

1 wants 2 to fight for his points and to stand up for what he believes. She has a hard time trusting that 2 will be able to stay focused and push forward when things get difficult.

From 2's point of view, it's rather different. 2 wants 1 to relax and stop attacking all of the time. He has a hard time trusting that 1 really cares about people.

Scenario #2

In Scenario #2, we examine what happens when someone with a *FIRE/WIND* orientation meets someone with a *WATER/GROUND* orientation.

PERSON 1 typically uses *moving into* and *moving away*.

PERSON 2 typically uses *moving back* and *not moving*.

PERSON 1   (FIRE/WIND)   says of 2   "She's too cautious."

PERSON 2   (WATER/GROUND)   says of 1   "He is impractical."

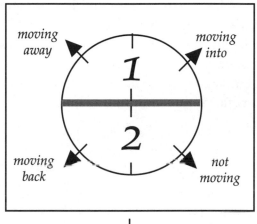

• likes ideas   • gets excited
• sees the big picture • is expressive

moving away — *moving into*

1

2

moving back — *not moving*

• feels the way   • likes details
• takes time   • is realistic

Figure 14–16.

1 wants 2 to just go for it. He feels that 2 gets caught up in the details and dampens her excitement by not trusting in the vision.

2 wants 1 to slow down and come back to earth. She feels that 1 gets caught up in the big picture and is not being realistic.

Which of these styles do you know the best?
Which of these styles do you know the least?

Where are you already strong (or too strong)?
Where are you not strong enough?

In light of what you want to be, where do you need to work?

IMAGINATION IN MOTION

The inherent tendency of a bureaucracy to defend itself against change is well documented. By relaxing its boundary sensitivity, we can encourage it to open to change. To achieve this aim we will be working one small step at a time so that your personal bureaucracy gets used to your experimentation and begins to accept your direction.

We have four exercises that are designed to promote the inner movement that is necessary if change is to occur. They will gently activate your habit defenses and give you the rare opportunity to observe a very deep layer of habit: the territorial and boundary responses that you learned in childhood. These unrecognized and tightly held reactions thicken the glue that binds us to our past. The new perceptions these exercises bring out can open a whole new horizon of possibilities.

Movement	*Ring*
not moving	*GROUND*
stepping back	*WATER*
stepping forward	*FIRE*
turning away	*WIND*

Exercise: **Responding with the Strategy of** *GROUND*

• Stand and activate Centered Presence.

Find . . . your feet
. . . your hands
. . . your head
. . . your breath

• Now imagine that someone you do not know
  is approaching.

• As they encounter your territorial boundary,
  use the energy of this moment to remember
  where you are and that you are not going to move.

• Let your weight sink to your feet and imagine that your
  outer boundaries are growing thicker and stronger.

• As the imaginary person touches your boundaries,
  see yourself resisting
  yet not actively fighting their attempt.

- Hold your position for a few seconds.

- Now return to Centered Presence.

As you repeat the exercise, pay special attention to what is happening to you as the imaginary person gets close.

> *What are you feeling?*
> *What internal dialogue is triggered?*
> *Where is the physical tension building up?*
> *How difficult was it to not move?*
> *How do you want to react?*

The *GROUND* response of **not moving** is a valuable ally in many different kinds of situations. It generates the strength to resist the pushes and the pulls of people and situations. *GROUND* does not come forward to meet the approaching force. It waits and responds only when necessary. It is as though the walls of your boundaries can thicken to repel the incoming force.

With the *GROUND* response, you trust in your power to resist and are free to relax internally, feeling safe and secure.

*The force bounces off
the solidity of your boundaries.*

Figure 14–17.

However, it is also possible to be too good at this strategy. There are two basic versions of excess of *GROUND*. One is to have so much boundary strength that nothing can get to you, no one can move you, and you cannot show how you feel.

The second version of excess of *GROUND* is the pseudoground of bureaucratic resistance. It fights any action that has the potential to change the system, thereby maintaining the status quo.

inherent
strength

bureaucractic
resistance

Figure 14–18.

*The strength and weakness of GROUND—**not moved**.*

Strengths	**Weaknesses**
decisive	needs results
powerful	afraid of failure
independent	needs to learn to listen
efficient	needs to express positive feedback
authoritative	
results-oriented	
persistent	

Exercise: **Responding with the Strategy of *WATER***

• Stand and activate Centered Presence.

Find . . . your feet
. . . your hands
. . . your head
. . . your breath

• Now imagine that someone you do not know is approaching.

- As they encounter your territorial boundary,
  use the energy of this moment to step backward.

- Imagine that in response to your stepping back,
  the imaginary person takes another step forward.

- In response to their continuing forward movement,
  step back again and again, matching their moves.

- At a certain point, the person stops and then turns and
  walks away.

- As they move away from you, move forward,
  back to where you were standing before the encounter.

- Now return to Centered Presence.

As you repeat the exercise, pay special attention to what is happening to you as the imaginary person gets close.

> *What are you feeling?*
> *What internal dialogue is triggered?*
> *Where is the physical tension building up?*
> *How difficult was it to step back?*
> *How do you want to react?*

The *WATER* response of **stepping back** creates the possibility for the strategic use of yielding. Built upon the organism's capacity for adaptation, elasticity, and resiliency, it is the response that is the least understood and valued in our culture. To help you to grasp this style, imagine the following scene. Someone is coming toward you. Like the *GROUND* response, you do nothing and wait for them to touch you. Instead of tightening your walls to resist them, you bend to accommodate their pressure. When the pressure builds up, and before your boundary is overwhelmed, you step backward.

WATER uses the incoming pressure to reshape its boundaries. This adaptation is achieved without any loss of boundary integrity. Once the person/pressure leaves, the boundaries return to their natural shape. This allows you to take an impression of the other person's actions, in other words, "I know you by how you change me."

adapt to the pressure

release the adaptation

Figure 14–19.

Yielding is often confused with the responses of giving up or giving in. These represent two of the commonly recognized but ineffective ways of using the *WATER* response. Beginning with the idea of an incoming pressure, we can view yielding as having two phases: *going back* and *coming forward again*.

The giving-in response goes back, but does not come forward again. You adapt to the pressure and when it releases, you continue to stay pushed back and stuck where you are. Imagine a piece of clay, which has the ability to adapt and be reshaped by the incoming force, but cannot by itself return to its original shape.

The giving-up response implies both the act of being reshaped and the act of losing your boundary integrity. It is more like submitting than yielding. When you give up you feel like your will is paralyzed. It is as though you open up your boundaries and let them in, even though you wanted to say no.

gives in

gives up

- adapts to the pressure
- does not return to Centered Presence

- submits to the pressure
- loses Centered Presence

Figure 14–20.

Yielding, done well, is like the action of a wave. It moves back from the shore and then it returns. In the martial art of T'ai Chi Ch'uan, which specializes in this response style, it is well recognized that by yielding you get the other person to reveal themselves, with both their strengths and their weaknesses. This is as valuable in fighting as it is in producing harmonious relationships.

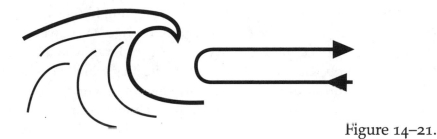

Figure 14–21.

The response of moving back from an encounter is subtly powerful. Yielding has a bad reputation in many quarters, for it is often done so poorly. This is especially true among people for whom going forward and making progress is of prime concern. Yielding or going backward is perceived as losing your momentum toward your goal.

The strength and weakness of WATER—*moved back.*

Strengths	Weaknesses
cooperative	needs harmony
considerate	afraid of rejection
likeable	needs to learn goal orientation
responsive	needs to express negatives
loyal	
emotional glue for team	

Dorothy: Session #4

The issue with which Dorothy had been wrestling was not an easy one. It has as much to do with society at large as it has to do with Dorothy herself. As long as power and femininity are seen as mutually exclusive, or at best, at odds with each other, then everyone, especially a woman in Dorothy's position, is hampered in the cultivation of their greatest abilities and contributions. In the language of strategy we are speaking of the inherent tension between the Ring of *FIRE* (= self-motivated, forward moving, penetrating power) and *WATER* (= other-oriented, backward moving, responsive power). Developing skill in working with this dynamic tension is a prerequisite for accessing true versatility.

From the point of view of the body, what might appear as semantic differences are real differences. Before designing her next practice, we asked Dorothy which was more important: 1. to be "powerful and caring" or 2. to be "caring and powerful." The order in which you perform your actions can have as potent an effect as which actions you choose to do. You wouldn't paint a new building before putting in the foundation. After some discussion, Dorothy chose to build her power upon her capacity for caring. She realized that she had always tried it the other way, and it had never worked.

Strategically, we wanted to assist Dorothy in cultivating the *FIRE* side of *WATER*. This is the image of a wave as it comes toward the shore. The power of this way of moving does not depend upon authoritative command ("You will get out of my way"). Therefore, it will not push that button in others. You get knocked over by the wave simply because you are standing in the way. It did not do it to you. If you were as strong as a mountain, the water would bounce off and return and bounce off again until you were washed away.

Before the wave comes forward to meet the shore, it first draws back. This is where Dorothy's new practice began. We taught her a basic *WATER* posture: 1. Stand with your right foot behind your left, but not directly behind the left, slightly off to the side (for better balance); 2. hold hands at chest height, with palms facing forward, and left hand in front of right; 3. the weight balance is 60 percent back leg and 40 percent front leg; 4. the palms are strong, like guardians of a gateway, and they give a little before springing back.

To make this more than just a physical exercise, we taught her the following inner exercise: 1. Inhale, tighten the lower belly, draw it back toward the spine, letting your weight shift 70 percent to the back leg, and then exhale, relax your belly and return to 60–40 balance. This cultivates the strength of the wave leaving the shore. 2. Inhale and press your palms forward to meet the shore, and exhale, letting the hands return to the starting point. 3. As you inhale, you begin to draw back with your belly and then you press forward with your palms as you continue shifting to your back leg. The message that is being written in your nervous system is: "I move back so I can move forward." Or, receptivity leads and power follows. We suggested that she practice this a minimum of ten minutes a day, five days a week for the next month.

Exercise: **Responding with the Strategy of *FIRE***

- Stand and activate Centered Presence.

**Find . . . your feet
. . . your hands
. . . your head
. . . your breath**

- Now imagine that someone you do not know is approaching.

- As they encounter your territorial boundary, use the energy of this moment to step forward to meet them.

- Now return to Centered Presence.

As you repeat the exercise, pay special attention to what is happening to you as the imaginary person gets close.

What are you feeling?
What internal dialogue is triggered?
Where is the physical tension building up?
How difficult was it to step forward?
How do you want to react?

The *FIRE* response of **stepping forward** is about meeting the incoming force, person, or event. Like the energy of magnetic attraction, it charges up the atmosphere of the encounter. We will examine two of the most important issues that can be learned through this style: spontaneity versus impulsiveness and penetrating versus fighting.

The difference between spontaneity and impulsiveness has to do with **timing.** How long do you wait before you respond to the person coming toward you? How close do they have to get to your territorial boundary before you respond?

Martial art masters tell us that spontaneous and appropriate responses are linked to the ability to **wait** to allow the whole body to perceive the situation before acting. When you react impulsively you have a diminished capacity for awareness, discrimination, and action. As soon as you become aware that you are acting impulsively, the appropriate strategy is to activate Centered Presence.

Another potential opportunity for learning lies in the distinction between fighting an obstacle that stands in your path and penetrating the resistance that it offers to your forward motion. The difference is in the way you interpret this obstacle/resistance.

From the natural perspective of *FIRE,* this obstacle that stands before me is *not* in my way. It is simply something I pass through **along the way.** When I think of it as something that is *in* my way, I find myself fighting it.

The *FIRE* response looks ahead, beyond the obvious obstacle, to the goal. This attitude or way of thinking transforms the entire encounter. That which was once an obstacle to your forward motion becomes something that you now pass through.

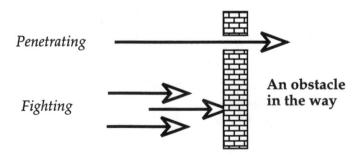

Figure 14–22.

*The strength and weakness of FIRE—**move into.***

Strengths	Weaknesses
inspirational	needs recognition
creative	afraid of not being enough
outgoing	needs to slow down
dramatic	needs to learn discipline
optimistic	afraid of not doing enough
competitive	
persuasive	

Exercise: **Responding with the Strategy of *WIND***

- Stand and activate Centered Presence.

Find . . . your feet
. . . your hands
. . . your head
. . . your breath

- Now imagine that someone you do not know
  is approaching.

- As they encounter your territorial boundary,
  use the energy of this moment to turn
  and step out of the way.

- Imagine that they continue moving past you,
  missing you completely.

- Now return to Centered Presence.

As you repeat the exercise, pay special attention to what is happening to you as the imaginary person gets close.

What are you feeling?
What internal dialogue is triggered?
Where is the physical tension building up?
How difficult was it to turn away?
How do you want to react?

The *WIND* response **turns out of the way** of the incoming force. *WIND* unlike *FIRE* does not move of its own accord. It waits to be acted upon. Unlike *GROUND*, it is unattached to its current position and even resists being touched. Unlike *WATER*, it does not bend.

Giving way to the incoming force is like being a leaf that does not resist the wind. Practicing this quality you cultivate an attitude of calm, like being in the eye of a storm. By learning to stay calm in the midst of turmoil, you can act with clarity and precision. Using the least amount of effort, martial artists are taught to redirect the blow rather than confront it directly.

turn yourself away

turn the other person aside

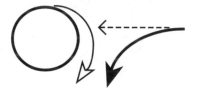

Figure 14–23.

When you cannot access the quality of calm amidst turmoil, the *WIND* response becomes one of paralysis and defenselessness coupled with the inability to access your power. This condition all too often leads to two well-known reaction styles: 1. letting go too much, "the space cadet;" or 2. fighting too hard to hold on, "the control freak." The space cadet gets blown away like the leaf. The control freak tries to overmanage all of the leaves.

The strength and weakness of WIND—*move away.*

Strengths	*Weaknesses*
thoughtful	needs perfection
unemotional	afraid of being wrong
data oriented	needs to learn to initiate
precise	needs to express emotions
systematic	needs to learn to risk
serious	
unaggressive	

Christopher: Session #4

Often our greatest gift is just the other side of our greatest weakness. From the point of view of the body, they are inseparably connected and reveal themselves in our every action. From his own reports and from our observation, the keys to Christopher's personal infrastructure were: 1. he was head oriented; 2. he liked to be in control; 3. it was difficult to move him off his position; 4. his body was tense; 5. when stressed, he got irritable, frustrated, and angry. In the language of strategy used by Miyamoto Musashi in *A Book of Five Rings,* Christopher was biased toward the negative side of the Rings of *WIND* and *GROUND* (*WIND* = have to be in control, angry; *GROUND* = tense, unmovable).

Strategically, the best time to interrupt the automaticity of Christopher's programming was just as his irritability was being activated and before he locked into his anger. That was the moment when the reactive side of *WIND* was being triggered. This was the lynch pin of his whole system. Once he got "pissed," his driving, analytical self took over, and that guy didn't stop for or notice anyone. *If* he were able to do something different —in other words, make a new response—in that key moment, then a truly different future would unfold.

The practice we taught Christopher was so deceptively simple that it took several demonstrations for him to even believe that it could work. It was based upon a positive use of the *WIND* strategy, in other words, ease, lightness, and circular movement. Christopher was asked to lift his hands out to the side at shoulder height with his palms and gaze turned slightly upward, and then to walk in a circle.

Once he learned the physical movement, we raised the stakes. First we asked him to imagine a situation that evoked an angry and analytical reaction. Staying with the upset he was to lift his hands and walk in a circle. To his amazement, the anger vanished, his calm center returned and he had just the right answer to the situation. Because he especially needed to access this skill in meetings, we ended the session by exploring ways of doing the move that looked less stylized and more ordinary.

15

RETOOLING YOUR PERSONAL STRATEGY

Pay attention even to trifles. Perceive those things which cannot be seen. Know the smallest things and the biggest things, the shallowest things and the deepest things.

— Miyamoto Musashi, *A Book of Five Rings*

DEEPENING YOUR ABILITY to notice the internal actions that sustain your habits is essential to the process of creating authentic change. Using the following exercises, you can awaken these perceptions within yourself. They expand your appreciation and skill in using the strategies of the Rings. The immediate effect is an enhanced ability to observe your habits *in action*. **They teach you how to purposefully reshape your muscular mind, so that it provides the environment for the quality you seek to spontaneously emerge.**

THE RING OF GROUND

Exercise: The *GROUND* Breath

- Stand with Centered Presence.
- Prepare to resist being moved from that spot.
- Breathe into your lower belly.
- Let the inhaled breath expand your abdomen.

- Allow the breath-energy to spread down your legs.
- Exhale with a gentle "Ahh."
- Repeat many times.

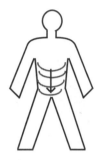

breathing
into your
lower belly

Figure 15–1.

The sound of "Ahh" is considered to be relaxing or even cleansing. If you explore the "Ahh" sound when you feel uptight and frustrated, you will find that it is hard to do in this state, but if you can do it, your muscles will soften and your mood will mellow.

"Ahh" shifts your energy downward, and that is the first step to finding GROUND. By practicing it when you "don't need it," you will have an easier time accessing it when you really do need it.

The belly breath is unfamiliar to most of us because of the stereotypical posture of our culture. Differences in culture are also differences in postural attitudes. Western culture with its historical emphasis on intellectual achievement and emotional expression has favored an upper-body posture—stomach in, chest up. Eastern culture, especially that of China and Japan, has favored a lower-body posture—chest and belly relaxed.

Opening and expanding the belly involves more than just learning a new muscular skill. It is also a challenge to your psyche. By paying careful attention as you perform this simple act, you may notice that as your lower belly begins to expand, your internal dialogue immediately shifts to "Oh no, I feel fat." This has obviously nothing to do with weight. It has more to do with advertising images and their internalized kinesthetic reflections.

If you can pass through this social defense, you will discover a world of stability, centeredness, and connection to nature that will radically alter your personal foundation. As your belly sense or feeling grows, you may find it more difficult to hold on to some of your familiar "problems."

Exercise: The *GROUND* Stance

- Stand with Centered Presence.

- Breathe into your lower belly, allowing your abdomen
  to expand on the inhale and contract on the exhale.

- Use the inhale to bring your hands up to your diaphragm,
  with wrists and fingers relaxed and
  palms pressing on an invisible beachball.

- As you exhale,
  bend your knees and
  turn your palms toward the floor,
  feeling your fingers and hands filling with quiet strength,
  as you move your hands downwards,
  as though on a 45-degree-angle ski slope,
  easing to a stop with elbows still slightly bent.

- As you inhale,
  straighten your legs as
  you bring your hands back to your diaphragm.

- As you exhale,
  release your hands and allow them to float back down.

- Repeat.

This exercise uses a simple gestural movement to assist you in accessing one of the major qualities of the Ring of *GROUND*. The arms and hands that you use to reach and to hold originally evolved to serve as your front legs. In a primordial way, they support your torso and help you move through the world.

Through the Ring of *GROUND*, you have access to your animal power. In the martial arts, you are taught to use your legs and hips to provide the strength for your punch. By imagining and feeling something tangible underneath your hands supporting them, your nervous system can relax downward to tap the wellspring of your inherent strength.

Another important learning that is encoded into this simple practice is the suggestion to bend your knees before moving your hands down the ski slope. By using this movement of your legs, you can more easily contain the power of the *GROUND*. When you couple this with the inner instruction, "no one can move my hands," a quiet strength is produced that will only show itself when someone tries to move you. There is no trace of struggle or fear, just calm power.

Anthony: Session #4

Anthony realized that he was at an impasse in his retooling adventure. When questioned in depth, he revealed that he had always distrusted and disapproved of "take charge" kind of people. His experience mirrored the natural tension that develops between the styles of *WATER* (= consensus oriented, gives way under pressure) and *GROUND* (= "This is what I want you do," resists being moved). He had developed the interpretation that *GROUND* oriented people had lost touch with their feelings and compassion. He was afraid that this would happen to him. He also felt that the *GROUND* style was overly fight oriented. "I do not like to fight," he declared.

We knew that unless we worked with this belief it was going to sabotage his efforts. We spoke of the many kinds of "fighting," some of which did produce the effects that he wished to avoid, and others that were more acceptable to him. In particular we explored the difference between fighting to defend your own boundaries versus taking the fight to someone else's territory. We used the image of a fort with its strong outer walls protecting the people within. He agreed that this was the quality of fight energy that he wanted to develop.

We taught Anthony an exercise that cultivates the strength and attitude of *GROUND without fighting.* The basic posture is: 1. take a wide stance with your right leg in front of left and slightly to the side (for stability), and 2. lift your hands to the level of your waist with palms facing down with the right hand in front of the left, in line with your right foot.

To empower this practice, Anthony learned two internal exercises. The first emphasizes breathing. The steps are: 1. find your feet and relax downward, 2. breathe into your lower belly, and 3. at the peak of your inhale, straighten and tighten your fingers. It takes a special kind of strength to resist without fighting. This exercise will cultivate it.

The second internal exercise emphasizes the power of a well-spo-ken declaration. As one of us approached Anthony and attempted to lift up his hand, he was to say to himself, clearly and strongly, "No one can pick up my hand." At that moment, he was to use his whole body's strength—tightening the muscles of his arms, abdomen, legs, and neck—to resist and to be unmovable. Once he learned the muscular signature of resisting without fighting, he was able to create imaginary opponents to work out with. He soon discovered that he was able to do this practice at work and no one could tell it wasn't "authentic."

Exercise: The *GROUND* Move

- Stand with Centered Presence,
  breathing into your lower belly.

- Inhale and bring your hands up to diaphragm height,
  wrists and fingers relaxed,
  palms supported by an invisible beachball.

- As you exhale, bend your knees and
  shift your weight onto your left leg.
  Step forward with the right foot.
  As you shift your weight onto the right leg, move your
  hands downward with the palms facing the floor.

- Feel your fingers and hands filling with quiet strength,
  as though on a 45-degree-angle ski slope,
  easing to a stop with elbows still slightly bent.

- Standing in the *GROUND* Stance,
  take several breaths and fill your whole body.

- Imagine a person in front of you
  and imagine that you can resist all of their force,
  with the strength of the walls of a fort.

- Inhale and shift your weight to your front leg.

- Exhale and step backward with your front foot,
  returning to the starting position.

- Relax your hands downward and
  return to standing with Centered Presence.

- Now do it with left foot and left hand leading.

- Repeat.

impassive gaze

*hands are
unmovable*

*breathe into
lower belly*

take a stand

Figure 15–2.

Questions for the *GROUND* Move

Did your feet lead your hands?

If your hands lead while making a *GROUND* move, then an overly aggressive tone or presence is produced. It is as though you feel like you have to fight for this position. This firelike solidity is unnecessary. This strategy is based upon the step-by-step natural unfoldment of intention into action and a trust in your own inherent strength.

While moving, did you feel stable or unsteady?

The essence and the practice of *GROUND* is to move from one stable position to another, without any breaks, like a mountain moving fluidly. Whenever too much of your attention draws inward and upward (to your head) while you are in the midst of this movement, unsteadiness will appear. It is a high art to remain solid while thinking, but it can be developed. The secret is to first cultivate a stable flow and then to explore thinking while moving. Every building begins with the construction of a foundation.

Were your hands really solid and strong?

There is an important martial arts saying that fits here: "You can know how you feel, but you cannot tell from that feeling how it will affect others." In other words, as you follow the instructions about bringing the hands forward and down, you might feel that they are solid and strong, but they may only be so in appearance, not in actuality.

We recommend that you enlist the support of a friend to test you while in the *GROUND* stance. Do not be surprised if 1. your hands are easily movable, or 2. you fight to hold them steady. Immediately thank your friend for providing you new insight into the workings of your bureaucracy. Go back to the beginning of this set of exercises and progressively build a new foundation to express your capacity for solidity and strength.

THE RING OF WATER

Exercise: The *WATER* Breath

- Stand with Centered Presence,
  open to being moved.

- Relax your chest, head, and shoulders.

- Relax your hips, knees, and belly.

- Breathe into your lower back.

- Let the inhale pull in your abdomen.

- Allow this movement to gently round your back.

- As you exhale, let your belly relax and
  your spine straighten.

- Repeat many times.

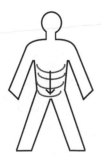

*breathing
into your
lower back*

Figure 15–3.

The key to this exercise is to **round your lower back as you inhale.** If you imagine that the force of the abdominal muscles moving back looks like the arrow in the diagram of the *WATER* move, then you can see that this practice duplicates the essence of *WATER*. The postural shape that is generated by the inhale is that of a bowl, with its opening turned toward the world.

The postural shape of the WATER breath

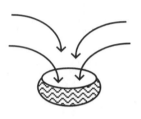

is also the shape of accepting and receiving.

Figure 15–4.

According to Jou Tsung Hwa in his encyclopedic *The Tao of T'ai Chi Ch'uan*, this practice is called "reverse" or "prenatal" breathing. It is said to imitate the general breathing pattern of the fetus in its mother's womb and is used to cultivate the strength to move against the current of habit and history. It is also used as a tonic to slow down and reverse the aging process.

Exercise: The *WATER* Stance

- Stand with Centered Presence.

- Inhale into your lower back
  and feel your abdomen pull in
  as you gently round your back.

- Exhale and let your belly relax and your spine straighten.

- Next, use the inhale to bring your hands up to chest height
  and let your wrists and fingers relax
  with your palms facing your chest.

- Use the exhale to bend your knees,
  turn your palms to face front and
  extend them forward
  as your hips move slightly backward.

- And when you inhale again,
  straighten your legs as you bring your hands
  back to your chest.

- Use the exhale to release your hands
  to float back downward.

- Repeat.

The *WATER* strategy has two complementary aspects. On one hand, you allow yourself to be moved back by the incoming person, situation, or force. On the other, you stay there to be touched by that which is coming toward you. Staying there to be touched makes a big difference.

before you move back,
first meet the incoming force

Figure 15–5.

Exercise: **The WATER Move**

- Stand with Centered Presence,
  breathing into your lower back.

- Inhale and bring your hands up to chest level,
  with your wrists and fingers relaxed and
  your palms facing your chest.

- As you exhale,
  bend your knees and shift your weight onto your left leg,
  step back with the right foot
  as you shift your weight onto the right leg,

turn your palms to face front,
and extend your arms forward
with the left hand 12 to 18 inches in front.

- Standing in the *WATER* Stance,
  take several breaths and fill your whole body.

- Imagine a person in front of you and
  imagine that you can receive and absorb all of their force.

- Inhale and shift your weight to your front leg.

- Exhale,
  step forward with your back foot
  and return to starting position

- Relax your hands downward and
  return to Centered Presence.

- Now do it with left foot and right hand leading.

- Repeat.

meet their gaze

*move hands forward
to touch*

*breathe into rounded
lower back*

step backward

Figure 15–6.

Questions for the *WATER* Move

Did your feet actually lead your hands?

If the hands lead while you are making a *WATER* move, then it is as
though you care more about the person who is coming toward you and
their responses to you than you do for yourself. Explore doing this exercise with feet leading and then hands leading. Notice the differences
in your internal conversations and mood.

Was your movement smooth or "jerky"?

Smoothness is one of the hallmarks of *WATER* done well. The behaviors of cooperation, responsiveness, and harmony that are associated with this style are akin to the capacity to flow with changes. If you practice bending your knees before shifting your weight onto your left leg before stepping back with the right foot before shifting your weight onto the right leg before turning your palms to face front, it will teach your nervous system **the timing of flow.**

THE RING OF FIRE

Exercise: **The *FIRE* Breath**

- Stand with Centered Presence.

- Prepare to move on purpose
  and not in response to anyone.

- Breathe into your chest,
  letting the inhale pick up your ribs.

- Allow your uplifted posture to lift your face into a smile.

- As you exhale, let your smile relax and your chest soften.

- Repeat.

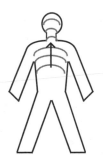

*breathing
into your
chest*

Figure 15–7.

The *FIRE* Breath exercise is designed to evoke the muscular quality associated with an uplifted spirit, an outgoing attitude, and a capacity to move into and through barriers. If you do not notice any experiential shifts from doing the exercise, try instead the time-tested and effective technique of "fake it till you make it."

Breathing up into your chest is the experiential correlate of lifting up your spirits. This practice generates an energy of excitement in the chest. The *FIRE* styles tend to live with a greater "charge" in their chests than do other styles. The secret to their creative, persuasive behavior is that in response to this excitement, they go forward joyfully into the situation. Other styles, in particular the *WIND*, pull away from this charge. This small internal act makes a big difference.

1st - let the breath fill your chest
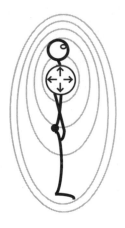
2nd - let the breath spread to fill your whole body

Figure 15–8.

**In the mood of joy,
the heart fills with energy,
which then spreads all throughout the body.**

**In the mood of joy,
expansion is the underlying state;
fear and anxiety have nothing to hold on to.**

If you wish to retool for more joy in your life, then take more time with the *FIRE* exercises.

Exercise: The *FIRE* Stance

- Stand with Centered Presence.

- Breathe into your chest,
  lifting your ribs on the inhale and
  relaxing them on the exhale.

- As you inhale,
  bring your hands up to chest height,
  wrists and fingers relaxed and
  with your palms facing your chest.

- As you exhale,
  straighten your fingers and
  move your hands forward,
  palms facing each other, 6 to 8 inches apart,
  stopping before your elbows straighten.

- As you inhale,
  bring your hands back to your chest.

- As you exhale,
  release your hands to float back down

- Repeat.

Compared to more "grounded" styles, the creative, inspirational, outgoing person reaches out to meet the world to express himself or herself and to cut through barriers or obstacles. This exercise is designed to shift your postural balance so that you are ready to meet the world from your chest *(heart)* and not from your head. Using your breath to support the movement encourages the authenticity of the act.

*extending yourself
in readiness to move
forward into the world*

Figure 15–9.

Working with the following questions will strengthen your ability to observe your habits in action. The exercise is designed to fit the *FIRE* way of doing things. If *FIRE* is not your normal way of operating, then you will probably feel that the movements are uncomfortable and strange. It is likely that your old habits will attempt to distort the movement to fit their familiar tone, rhythm, or direction.

> *How are you reaching forward internally as you are reaching forward externally, through space?*
>
> *Are your fingers fully straightening or are they still partially bent?*
>
> *Are your hands coming together or are they separating as they move out?*
>
> *Are you overextending your elbows?*

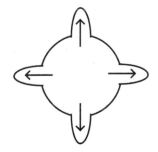

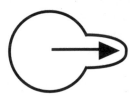

hands too far apart = diffuse focus

hands too close together = overly focused

Figure 15–10.

Pauline: Session #4

No amount of practice was going to convince Pauline that *down* was where she wanted to be. It just didn't have the kind of excitement that she wanted in her life. However, after several months of training it was no longer the enemy. Now that her *up* was not defined by her rejection of *down*, the next step was to develop an exciting, focused, unstoppable, and powerfully solid *up*. In the language of strategy, this is a *FIRE-GROUND* combination.

For the warrior, movement is potent medicine. The master watching you perform your exercises does not see a body in motion, he or she sees a life in motion. How you feel, what you believe, what you have learned in the past, what motivates you, all these are considered to be present, in every movement you make, in every realm of your life. It is from this paradigm that we taught Pauline a form that is used to cultivate *FIRE* with *GROUND*.

The basic mechanics of the form are: 1. stand erect, with the left foot in front of the right, with the left arm leading; 2. hold both hands at solar plexus height; 3. hands are filled with dynamic tension, with fingers almost fully extended and pointed approximately 20 to 30 degrees upward. The movement itself is simple: the back hand (the right) comes forward, and the back foot (the right) follows until you have returned to the starting position, although on other side. But, this was just the external side of Pauline's new practice.

The internal exercise Pauline learned was based upon Centered Presence. Standing in the posture, 1. relax your torso and jaw and feel it flow down into your feet; 2. see in your mind's eye a goal that you want to attain and then let your torso relax upward, slightly straightening your legs; 3. **want** to reach for it, to push through any obstacle in your path, grab it, and then bring it toward you; 4. move your back hand forward and take a step.

By consciously working with the internal actions of grounding, envisioning, and wanting, Pauline was building a new foundation, one that would support her in being more exciting, focused, unstoppable, and powerfully solid.

Exercise: The *FIRE* Move

- Stand with Centered Presence, breathing into your chest.

- Inhale and bring your hands up to chest level,
   with your wrists and fingers relaxed and
   your palms facing your chest.

- Exhale,
   move your hands forward, with your right hand leading
   and with your fingers straight,
   as though you could cut straight through,
   and you let your right foot follow your hands into a step.

- Standing in the *FIRE* Stance,
  take several breaths and fill your whole body.

- Imagine a person in front of you as being
  "along the way but not *in* the way."

- Inhale,
  bringing your hands back to the chest and
  shifting your weight to your back leg.

- Exhale,
  relax your hands downward,
  bringing your front foot back,
  and return to standing with Centered Presence.

- Now do it with left hand and foot leading.

- Repeat.

look beyond

cut through

breathe up

step forward

Figure 15–11.

Questions for the *FIRE* Move

Did your hands actually lead your feet?

The timing of hands leading feet evokes a lighter mood than feet leading hands. Try it and you'll see what we mean. The naturally expressive person has this lightness of being.

Did you take a long step or a short one?

If you are stepping out far, ask yourself, "Do I overextend myself in life in general?" If you are taking very small steps, ask yourself, "Am I overly cautious?"

Did your chest move with the movement?

FIRE style people seem to get excited by and even thrive on what could be called anxiety. This is a feeling state that centers in the chest area. Holding your chest down as you step forward is a method for containing this feeling. Explore the difference. If you want to be more expressive, then you will have to reframe your interpretation of this energy.

THE RING OF WIND

Exercise: The *WIND* Breath

- Stand with Centered Presence.

- Prepare to get out of the way of the encounter.

- Breathe into your upper back.

- Let the inhale pick up your shoulders as your weight shifts to your heels.

- Exhale and let your shoulders relax and your balance shift forward.

- Repeat many times.

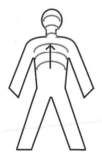

breathing into your upper back

Figure 15–12.

The *WIND* style is prone to thinking. If you were asked to point to the region of the body that is most involved with this type of action, you would point to the head. There are many types of thinking. One of the most common is "objective" thinking. This requires an attitude of relative detachment from what is going on.

The secret to being detached is to not let anything touch you. You simply move out of the way so that you can observe the play of action. This is a very important skill. This is also a skill that is overdeveloped in many people. You can get so good at it that you have trouble letting anything touch you, even if you want to have it happen.

Another sign of excess *WIND* is becoming "touchy" and easily triggered when your stress level rises and the tension backs up into your shoulders and head. It is as though the head, the neck, and the shoulders fuse into one tight bundle of discomfort.

The *WIND* Breath exercise is designed to work directly with this issue. The instruction "Let the inhale pick up your shoulders" is designed to activate on purpose and in a nonstressful way the same lifting up of the shoulders that gets triggered in the startle reflex. Through gentle repetition, the layers of built-up tensions can be washed away.

**By allowing yourself to touch yourself through the breath,
you are also opening the way for others to touch you.**

Exercise: The *WIND* Stance

- Stand with Centered Presence.

- Breathe into your upper back,
  inhaling and lifting your shoulders and
  shifting your balance back, then
  exhaling and relax your shoulders down and
  shifting your balance to the middle.

- Next, use the inhale to
  bring your hands up to chest height,
  with your wrists and fingers relaxed and
  your fingers pointed toward the ground.

- Use the exhale to
  spread your arms apart to the sides,
  palms facing upward,
  and feel free to rock back and forth on your feet.

- When you inhale again,
  bring your hands back to your chest.

- Use the exhale to release your hands to float back down.

- Repeat

When you stand with your arms spread apart, palms facing upward, so light on your feet that you can easily rock back and forth, it implies an attitude of nonresistance to whatever may happen. If you are not used to being this way, it can seem almost as if you are utterly defenseless. The difference lies in your legs. If you were to assume the attitude of open arms and at the same time hold to your position in space—in other words, refuse to move your feet—then you would be vulnerable to any attacker. However, this is not so if you are standing lightly on your feet. You can explore the difference by switching between these two stances.

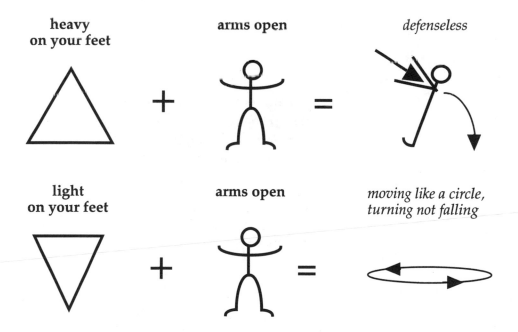

heavy on your feet   **arms open**   *defenseless*

light on your feet   **arms open**   *moving like a circle, turning not falling*

Figure 15–13.

To be **heavy on your feet** is to hold on stubbornly to your point of view until you feel that you have to submit or fight for your life.

To be **light on your feet** is to be able to accept a challenge to your intellectual position and to change your mind, when and if it is appropriate.

In the second case, giving up is not losing. It is an opportunity to get even clearer. In the first, giving up is losing everything. When you next find yourself in this situation, remember the two different movements. Choose the reality in which you wish to live. Do so by altering the weight load on your feet.

Exercise: **The *WIND* Move**

- Stand with Centered Presence,
  breathing into your upper back.

- Inhale and lift your shoulders and shift your weight back
  as you bring your hands up to chest level,
  wrists and fingers relaxed and
  fingers pointed toward the ground.

- Exhale,
  look to the left,
  spreading your arms open with palms facing upward
  as you turn and step back
  with your left foot and then the right
  to land at right angles to the "line of attack."

It's coming at you

It's going by you

Figure 15–14.

- Standing in the *WIND* Stance,
  take several breaths and fill your whole body.

- Imagine a person moving by you, but unable to touch you.

- Inhale,
  bring your hands back to the chest and
  turn your head to the right.

- Exhale,
  relax your hands downward as you turn and
  step with your left foot and then your right,
  so that you are standing where you began,
  with Centered Presence.

- Now do it by looking to the right
  with your right foot leading.

- Repeat.

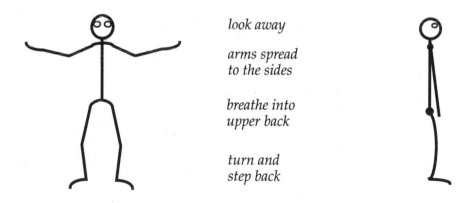

look away

*arms spread
to the sides*

*breathe into
upper back*

*turn and
step back*

Figure 15–15.

Questions for the *WIND* Move

Did you shift your weight back before moving?

Keeping your weight forward while lifting your shoulders places you in a dangerous position. Moving like this creates a split in your field of presence and action. In between the "up" generated by the shoulders and the "down" generated by not shifting back, a zone of undefendable openness forms.

shoulders up

excess of openness

weight forward

Figure 15–16.

As we said earlier, *WIND* has two faces. One response to this excess of openness is to feel weak and powerless. The other is to gird the loins of your ego and prepare to fight for your position. Neither of these is optimal, and they only come into existence when you split yourself in two.

Did your head lead the movement?

One of the purposes of this type of exercise is to communicate a sense of order and alignment to your nervous system. Lack of clarity and confusion can easily push your bureaucratic defenses into overload, producing a literal confusion in the brain-muscle connection. Faced by the need to get away and escape, precision and coordination are sacrificed.

PURSUING
YOUR VISION

16

SELF-MASTERY AND LEADERSHIP

Leadership and learning are indispensable to each other.
—John F. Kennedy

WE ALL HAVE visions of what we are to become. The passage from where we are *now* to where we want to be can be achieved by retooling our habits of action. To deal effectively with the changes that are facing us, we need to remember that *we* must change if we want to see a change in the world. Developing our personal skills to the fullest is an essential step toward a safe and prosperous future for all of us.

Our professional and personal worlds are interconnected. What we develop *within* us can be actualized in the world *around* us. By acting as a whole, we can radically enhance our performance in life and work. When we can work at a new level inside ourselves, we can make it work in a new way on the outside.

Our true inner strength emerges when we act as a whole, for in our essence we are whole. Growing up, we were neither trained nor told of the possibility of acting as a whole. We learned to be smaller than we are. We learned to be more fragmented than we are. Working with the dynamics of wholeness, we can grow into our full selves.

Each of us is a vital contributor to the group effort to solve our social and planetary problems. As you grow in awareness and power, so too grows your responsibility to act impeccably. Living and acting consonant with your values is critical, both to attain your personal goals and to serve the larger community. The most powerful behavior is focused by principles and guided by values.

Authentic and lasting change has never been an easy task to achieve. The most important and most difficult challenge you face is the battle with yourself, with how you do *not* walk your talk. The real enemy to change lies hidden within, wherever you cannot face the truth of your choices and your actions.

The fear of losing what you have can overpower your desire to achieve what you truly want. Imagine an aerial artist on the high-wire trapeze. At some point the performer must let go of the bar to reach for the bar that is the goal. If you don't let go of the first bar, you cannot get to the second.

Real leaders have the courage and willingness to address their inner fears. The most effective leaders are those who have resolved this inner battle and have aligned their deeper values with their external actions.

> *He who gains a victory over other men is strong, but he who gains a victory over himself is all powerful.*
>
> —Lao Tzu, *Tao Te Ching*

The power to work with change is one of the highest forms of mastery. Leaders work with everchanging sets of circumstances, people, and forces, seeking to produce optimal outcomes. Mastery of the change process and accomplishment go hand in hand. True masters of the change process know *both* the external and internal worlds.

The most powerful method to learn how to get the best from others is to learn how to get the best from yourself. What you learn in the process of mastering yourself has an immediate and powerful impact upon how you manage tasks and people. As a leader, one of your primary responsibilities is to get the best out of others. When we get the best from ourselves we become powerful role models, likely to evoke comparable excellence from our team.

You have the greatest leverage for change in working with your personal habits of action. Task and relationship depend on others or the world. Self-mastery begins with you. It is the most natural starting point for mastering your work in the world. The essence of self-mastery is wholeness-in-action.

Ironically, cultivating self-mastery receives the least amount of attention and study in the world of work. Since it is the least familiar, it offers the greatest potential increase in learning.

We need to create a culture that supports the rituals and practices of wholeness-in-action. We need to make heroes of those who cultivate their wholeness. We need to reward demonstrations of whole systems thinking and acting. We must seek our wholeness so that we can fulfill our individual and collective potential. We must recognize and understand how we have become fragmented.

People seek wisdom to do right action in the world. Wisdom can be found outside ourselves only temporarily. Eventually we must find wisdom from within. In other words, we must develop ourselves as an instrument that can access and hold wisdom. Wisdom is more than knowledge. Wisdom emerges from an experiential understanding of the principles that shape human experience. It is the discrimination that guides us in our moments of loss and confusion. It is the deep sense of guidance and trust we call upon in encounters with the unknown.

To continually refine your gifts is the challenge and joy of being a leader. The demonstration of this refinement reveals itself in the dynamic **balance** of what appear to be irreconcilable opposites: professional and personal life, power and love, accomplishment and relationship.

> *The most important thing in life is to have a great aim and to possess the aptitude and perseverance to attain it.*
>
> —Goethe

We encourage you to risk. What you can gain far outweighs what you might lose. Accomplishment takes work and commitment. If you are already successful, you already have this. The risk of living without risk may be the greatest danger of all.

What is possible is far greater than you imagine.

17

SUMMARY OF
ESSENTIAL EXERCISES

*One movement done consciously
is worth ten done unconsciously.*
—Arnold Schwarzenegger

**The more of yourself that you put into your actions,
the quicker you will reach your goal.**

IN THE MIDST of thinking about what to do, tune-in to what your feelings have to contribute. In the midst of a moment of intense emotional reactivity, notice your posture. In the midst of your everyday, ordinary, actions, check-in and discover what you are really thinking.

THE HEART OF RETOOLING:
ELEVEN KEY EXERCISES

1. Centered Presence

2. Using Centered Presence in Daily Life

3. Breathing your Way to Greater Control and
   More Spontaneity

4. Getting Unstuck from your Habits of Feeling

5. Relaxation in Action

257

6. Releasing Unwanted Tension and
   Shifting out of Negative Feelings

7. Cultivating the Ring of *GROUND*

8. Cultivating the Ring of *WATER*

9. Cultivating the Ring of *FIRE*

10. Cultivating the Ring of *WIND*

11. Cultivating Versatility and the Ring of *SPACE*

CREATING AN INDIVIDUALIZED TRAINING

The exercises are numbered only for convenience. You can do them in any order. For a well-balanced and comprehensive workout, we recommend doing all eleven exercises, at least once a week.

To assist you in developing a personal training, here are some suggested menus

	Exercises
• the basic training	1, 2
• basic change skills	3, 4, 5, 6
• cultivating versatility	7, 8, 9, 10, 11
• getting the most out of relaxation	5, 6
• working with your feelings	4, 6
• training for control/spontaneity	3, 7

If you wish to cultivate specific qualities, we have provided a self-assessment checklist and a Five Rings summary score sheet. Your responses to the instrument will focus your attention on the appropriate exercise (#7–11).

Practice makes perfect.

Lasting change is like a tree;
it starts small but if fed grows large and fruitful.

A Personal Retooling Self-Assessment

I want to be more ...

☐ decisive   ☐ powerful   ☐ independent

☐ efficient   ☐ authoritative   ☐ results-oriented

☐ cooperative   ☐ considerate   ☐ likeable

☐ responsive   ☐ team player   ☐ loyal

☐ inspirational   ☐ outgoing   ☐ dramatic

☐ optimistic   ☐ competitive   ☐ persuasive

☐ thoughtful   ☐ unemotional   ☐ logical

☐ precise   ☐ systematic   ☐ unaggressive

☐ happy   ☐ peaceful   ☐ appreciative

☐ calm   ☐ able to listen   ☐ harmonious

☐ balanced   ☐ goal oriented   ☐ able to slow down

☐ disciplined   ☐ of a risk taker   ☐ able to say yes

☐ able to say no   ☐ versatile   ☐ emotionally expressive

☐ _____   ☐ _____

I want to be less ...

☐ anxious   ☐ impatient   ☐ panicked   ☐ confused

☐ angry   ☐ frustrated   ☐ bored   ☐ depressed

☐ sad   ☐ afraid   ☐ worried   ☐ mind wandering

☐ empty   ☐ isolated   ☐ needy   ☐ afraid of failure

☐ giving in   ☐ giving up   ☐ holding on   ☐ unable to stop

☐ afraid of rejection   ☐ needy for recognition

☐ perfectionist   ☐ concerned with not being enough

☐ concerned with not doing enough   ☐ afraid of being wrong

☐ _____   ☐ _____

☐ _____

259

A Five Rings Summary Score Sheet

Transfer the results of the self-assessment to the chart below. Underline or circle the qualities that you wanted more of or less of. With an *isn't that interesting?* attitude, look for patterns. You might discover that all of your choices are clustered into one ring, what you want more of is clustered in one ring and what you want less of is clustered in another, or, there may not be a clearcut pattern.

Since this is not a test but a springboard for your personal exploration, use what you discover as an opportunity to begin. The exercises themselves will reveal where you have to go next.

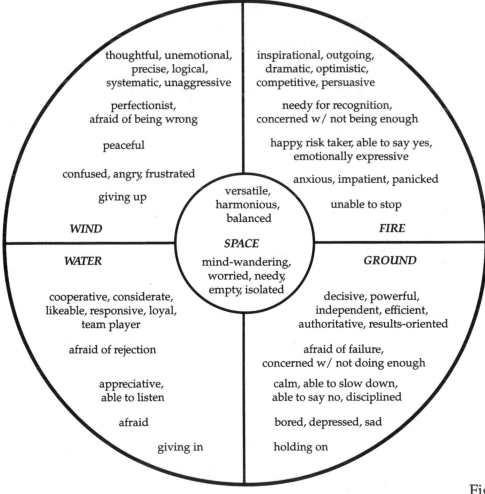

Figure 17–1.

1. Centered Presence

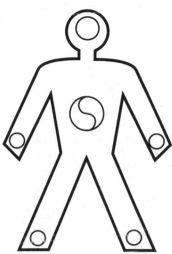

- **Find your feet.**

    Feel them touching the floor.

    Relax your face and mouth.

    Let your shoulders drop.

    Take a breath and exhale, saying, "Ahhhh."

    Soften your belly.

- **Find your hands.**

    Use your tactile senses to feel
    what you are touching.

    Notice the pressure and the contact.

    Take a breath and exhale, saying, "Ohhh."

    Use this new energy to soften your chest and your groin.

- **Find your head.**

    Use your eyes and look to see where you are.

    Use your ears and listen to what is being said.

    Notice how your head balances on the top of the spine.

    Take a breath and exhale, saying, "Ah ha!"

    Use this new energy to straighten up.

    Take the time for your muscles to shift and
    your mood to alter.

Figure 17–2.

**Centered Presence is the indispensable key for retooling
your personal infrastructure into an instrument
that can accomplish your goals.**

2. Using Centered Presence in Daily Life

As you progress in your practice of Centered Practice, you will discover yourself becoming more:

- grounded, solid, and stable
- connected, sensitive, and flexible
- alert, balanced, and coordinated
- spontaneous, controlled, and flowing

Figure 17–3.

1. **remember** to include your whole body in your awareness as you engage in your daily activities;

2. **pause** for an instant, in the midst of the goings-on, to let the instructions— *find your feet, hands, head and breath* — activate your muscles and affect your breathing;

3. **relax** the muscles that are maintaining your focus. (For example, if you are driving ahead with your will, look for excess tension in your face and forehead. If you realize that you are in a reactive mood, then try softening the muscles of your abdomen.);

4. **Say** the instructions again and encourage your muscles to respond to the words. Notice the small shifts as muscle-tension moves down to your feet, out to your hands and up to your head;

5. **Return** to whatever you are doing.

3. Breathing Your Way to Greater Control and More Spontaneity

Your patterns of experience and behavior are mirrored in the rhythms of your breath.

As long as your breathing rhythm stays the same, real change is difficult.

Every different way of being has its own way of breathing.

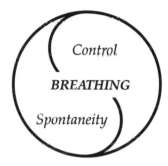

Figure 17-4.

To Cultivate Control

- Inhale and exhale—slowly and purposefully.
- Consciously pay attention to and smooth the transitions between the inhale and the exhale.

To Cultivate Spontaneity

- At the end of your next exhale—pause and wait for the inhale to happen.
- Do not try to breathe and do not hold your breath.
- Send messages of relaxation to your torso and throat.
- Do not force the breath, let it emerge in its own way— without judging it.
- Let your breath find its own rhythm.

4. Getting Unstuck from your Habits of Feeling

Posture shapes feeling which in turn shapes posture. Since every feeling is different, its corresponding muscular tension pattern is also different.

Moving into a new future is easier when you less muscularly tied to your old interpretations and experiences. By activating a familiar feeling state on purpose—without the usual external triggers—you can loosen its muscular grasp.

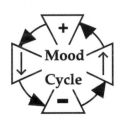

Figure 17–5.

- Evoke the feelings associated with the **positive** phase of your Mood Cycle.

  Let your muscles shift to fit it.

  Return to Centered Presence.

- Evoke the feelings associated with the **losing the positive** phase.

  Let your muscles shift to fit it.

  Return to Centered Presence.

- Evoke the feelings associated with the **negative** phase of your Mood Cycle.

  Let your muscles shift to fit it.

  Return to Centered Presence.

- Evoke the feelings associated with the **leaving the negative** phase.

  Let your muscles shift to fit it.

  Return to Centered Presence.

**By making the Mood Cycle into a conscious practice,
your bureaucracy's hold on you is weakened
and you are freer to creatively respond.**

5. Relaxation in Action

Authentic change is a process that involves the concrete reshaping of the whole system. Adding on new actions before letting go of old tensions results in just another layer that is added to your bureaucracy. The trick is to let go of what you no longer need while you are engaged in daily life.

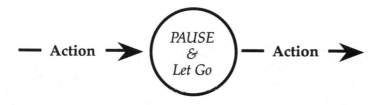

Figure 17–6.

- Slowly and easily sit and stand.

- In the midst of the movement, make many **mini-pauses.**

- With each pause remind yourself to:
  let go of what you do not need to be where you are now.

- Continue to move and pause,
  and then move and pause again.

Figure 17–7.

Each time you direct yourself to let go, let it go deep. Allow yourself time for the muscular movement of relaxation to get started and to build up momentum. You can use this method with every action.

6. Releasing Unwanted Tension and Shifting out of Negative Feelings

This exercise synthesizes the principles and skills developed in the prior exercises. By combining the ability to relax with the ability to recognize the feeling/muscle relationship, you can reach under your intellectual mind and literally reshape your pattern.

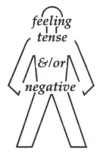

notice your mood/posture

feel the tight muscles

stretch them with your breath

return to Centered Presence

Figure 17–8.

- Notice your mood and your posture.
  Do you feel muscularly tense and/or is your mood negative?

- Scan your body for the points of maximum muscle tension.

- Focus your body-attention on the tension point that stands out the most.

- While holding your focus on this spot, relax the rest of your body.

- Gently breathe into this field of tension, energizing, and accentuating your experience of the tension.

- As you continue to breathe into this spot, use your inhale to stretch this tension field to reach: 1. your feet; 2. feet and hands; and 3. feet, hands, and head.

- Let go of the point you are holding in your attention and return to Centered Presence.

7. Cultivating GROUND

The ability to access the power of *GROUND* is necessary if you are to be

- able to make a stand and hold your position
- seen as a strong and decisive leader
- patient and calm

Figure 17–9.

The *GROUND* Attitude

- Stand with Centered Presence.
- Hold the desire to stay just where you are.
- Say "no!" to any attempt to move you.
- Wait until it is time to move.

The *GROUND* Posture

- Breathe into your lower belly.
- Gesture forward and down, with strength in your hands.
- Place your weight on your front foot.
- Remember the position you are holding—verbal or spatial

8. Cultivating WATER

The ability to access the power of *WATER* is necessary if you are to be

- able to stay in relationship even under stress
- seen as caring, adaptable and a good listener
- responsive and flowing

Figure 17–10.

The *WATER* Attitude

- Stand with Centered Presence.
- Have no desire to go anywhere in particular.
- Say "yes!" to the possibility of being moved by what you encounter.
- Allow yourself to be moved as though nothing can hurt you.

The *WATER* Posture

- Breathe into your lower back.
- Gesture with your palms facing forward.
- Place your weight on your back foot.
- Let the other person move you.

9. Cultivating FIRE

The ability to access the power of *FIRE* is necessary if you are to be

- able to move forward into any situation

- seen as inspirational, friendly and persuasive

- joyful and optimistic

Figure 17–11.

The *FIRE* Attitude

- Stand with Centered Presence.

- See in your mind's eye where you want to go.

- Say "yes" to this vision with your whole body.

- Move as though nothing can stop you.

The *FIRE* Posture

- Breathe into your chest.

- Gesture forward and up, with energy in your fingers.

- Place your weight on your front foot.

- Move forward into the situation with a positive attitude.

10. Cultivating WIND

The ability to access the power of *WIND* is necessary if you are to

- be able to let go of your position without loss of integrity
- be seen as thoughtful, perceptive and clear
- be detached and peaceful

Figure 17–12.

The *WIND* Attitude

- Stand with Centered Presence.
- Be willing to let go of your position.
- Say "no!" to any attempt to touch you.
- Wait until someone gets close and then move out of the way.

The *WIND* Posture

- Breathe into your upper back.
- Gesture with arms spread to the sides.
- Stand lightly on your feet.
- Be prepared to let go of your position.

11. Cultivating Versatility and the Ring of SPACE

The ability to access the power of versatility is necessary if you are to be

- consciously creative

- natural and authentic in a variety of styles

- powerful in a wide range of situations

- effective with individuals who embody different styles

GROUND   WATER   FIRE   WIND

Figure 17–13.

- Start with Centered Presence and shift into *GROUND*

- Return to Centered Presence and shift into *WATER*

- Return to Centered Presence and shift into *FIRE*

- Return to Centered Presence and shift into *WIND*

- Return to Centered Presence.

- For the following work-out patterns,
  return to Centered Presence after each shift.

  FIRE, WATER, WIND, and *GROUND*

  GROUND, FIRE, WIND, and *WATER*

  WATER, WIND, FIRE, and *GROUND*

- Notice what is different in your experience
  after each different work-out.

18

SUMMARY OF
ESSENTIAL IDEAS

Change is constant.

Everything is always changing. The world is changing and so are we. While change has always been considered important, it is now becoming the dominant factor in the cultural and economic landscape.

When you hold the "change as constant" paradigm, new possibilities and strategies emerge where there were obstacles and dead ends before. Actions based upon the fundamental nature of change lead to more powerful results.

We are living in a time when "change" is also accelerating. When you view change as a disruption, then the increasing rate of change creates the experience of future shock. When you navigate from the perspective that change is constant, less stress and confusion are produced.

Continuous learning is the optimal strategy for responding to the constancy of change.

Whenever you stop learning, you are operating as though the patterns you built in the past are sufficient to handle the future. When you stop learning, you begin to rigidify.

If you do not recognize or act upon the need for continuous learning, you bring about a future that is the same as the past. Are you willing to take the chance?

You are the first organization you must master.

To truly understand and master the changing world, you must first understand and master yourself in action. Standing between your intent to act and your action are your habitual patterns of self-organization. Intention manifests through self-organization.

The stumbling blocks to fulfillment are the unrecognized patterns of self-organization. These patterns are what you do to do what you do. The desire to be a vigilant observer of your personal behavioral patterns is one of the essential attitudes for someone who is interested in accomplishment.

Results are a function of the way you organize and use yourself. Your inner organization influences the tone and effectiveness of your actions.

The human capacity to learn is a double-edged sword.

Learning can work for you or against you. Once you have learned one way of performing a task, you encounter resistance when you try to do it any other way. This is especially true when you perceive yourself as doing it well or being successful. Our habits are potential deterrents to new learning. They produce predictable responses to new events.

All habits have limits. Are you aware of the limits of your habitual methods? The highest level of success and mastery comes from moving through our limiting factors.

If you don't watch out, you are going to end up where you are headed.

The personal bureaucracy is what we call the function of the neuromuscular system that allows us to perform recurrent tasks without having to pay conscious attention to what we are doing. It allows you to go through your day without having to pay conscious attention to the details of each activity, such as driving the car, eating, or dressing.

Bureaucracies are conservative. The bureaucracy contains our learned responses to change, stress, competition, and encounters in general. It is not their job to find new responses.

All learning is encoded in your body. All learning has five components: attention, feeling, thought, movement and posture. For example, your body remembers the mood and thoughts you had when you first learned a particular task. Successful change requires that you work with all these components.

If you want to fulfill your potential for accomplishment,
you must retool your habits of action and perception.

New skills require new habits. For new learning to be embodied, an actual change must occur in your personal bureaucracy. The key to producing lasting changes lies in building new habits.

There are three internal actions necessary for making changes in your personal infrastructure

1. **letting go** of what is no longer needed

2. **keeping** what still works

3. **adding on** whatever is missing

Applying traditional retooling strategy to our own lives
takes more time than is practical.

It is impractical to take time off from work to study. Lack of time creates the magnetism of the quick fix, which is the dream of big results in little time. Quick fixes do not last. They can only be superficial or, at best, lead to insights that need support or follow-up.

The secret to producing sustainable change is to work with
your behavioral foundation.

The most common mistake is to try to change your behavior without shifting the *foundation* of your personal bureaucracy. Most efforts fail due to inconsistent commitment and a lack of well designed effort.

The retooling on the run approach is to learn new action-habits while maintaining one's daily responsibilities. There are four strategic keys that will support your capacity to make sustainable changes.

1. Use every daily activity as the training ground for your learning.

2. Consciously shift your attention between what you are doing, externally, in the world, and what you are doing, internally, to organize yourself to accomplish that activity.

3. Consciously increase your awareness of the habitual internal actions you make during the course of your daily activities.

4. Learn to cultivate Centered Presence as a touchstone in the midst of action.

The practice of Centered Presence creates a new ground for positive habits.

By practicing Centered Presence in the midst of simple acts, such as standing, sitting, or walking, you will cultivate the skill to extend it to more complex activities, such as talking, writing, or meeting with people. Over time, wholeness-in-action becomes the new norm.

The long-term goal of Retooling on the Run is intentional versatility, the capacity to choose your action style in response to encounters. The ability to make purposeful shifts in your presence is one of the measures of personal power.

The best time to start is now.

Every moment is an opportunity to study change. Let yourself be guided by your intention to make a difference.

Chapter 1

1. Epstein, Seymour. "Anxiety and Learning." Unpublished paper. University of Massachusetts, 1966.

Chapter 3

1. Mehrabian, Albert. *Nonverbal Communication*. Chicago: Aldine-Atherton, Inc., 1972.

2. Gottlieb, Raymond, Ph.D., O.D., personal communication

Chapter 5

1. Maisel, Edward, ed., *The Resurrection of the Body—The Writings of F. Matthias Alexander*. New York: Delta, 1969. p. 17.

Chapter 11

1. Whatmore, George, and Kohli, Daniel. *The Physiopathology and Treatment of Function Disorders*. New York: Grune & Stratton, Inc., 1980.

Section V

1. Frager, Robert, ed., *Who am I? Psychological Types for Self-Discovery*. New York: Tarcher/Putnam, 1994.

Chapter 14

1. Frager, Robert, ed., *Who am I? Psychological Types for Self-Discovery*. New York: Tarcher/Putnam, 1994.

David Sheppard Surrenda, Ph.D.

DAVID SURRENDA is a licensed psychologist who has been performing executive level organizational consulting with business, government, education and health systems for twenty-four years.

He is the Director of The Leadership Edge, a group specializing in the challenges of executive leadership. It provides training and consultation to assist with strategic planning, leadership transitions, team building, executive coaching, conflict resolution and creative problem solving. He has consulted with and trained executives in over 100 national and international organizations including Apple Computer, Sun Microsystems, Applied Materials, British Petroleum, International Business Systems, Caesar's Resorts, and Merrill Lynch. He served for two years as a Chairman of a Los Angeles-based TEC (The Executive Committee) group, CEOs who provide training, support and consultation to one another in the management of their companies.

Mr. Surrenda founded the Graduate School for Holistic Studies at John F. Kennedy University in Orinda, California, and served as Graduate Dean there for nine years. He taught at JFKU in Management, Psychology, and Liberal Arts.

Mr. Surrenda has developed nationally distributed criminal justice programs in conflict resolution and crisis management. A film maker who has made three documentaries, he has directed nine major professional conferences and co-authored three books on conflict resolution.

Stuart Heller, Ph.D., 6th Dan

STUART HELLER has been studying kung fu, the art of excellence in action, for over thirty years and has been teaching for twenty. He earned sixth-degree black belts in two arts, Kempo Karate and Chinese Kempo.

After earning a bachelor's degree in mathematics, a master's degree in operations research and a doctoral degree in psychology and health systems science, he became certified as a hypnotherapist and a teacher of the F. M. Alexander Technique.

His consulting clients include executives and teams from McDonald's, NutraSweet, Apple Computer, The Los Angeles Police Academy, First National Bank of Chicago, Harvard Community Health Plan, and The Executive Committee (TEC). Mr. Heller developed the movement psychology specialization for the first accredited master's degree program in Clinical Holistic Health Education while a professor at John F. Kennedy University's Graduate School for Holistic Studies from 1979–1988.

The author of *The Dance of Becoming: Living Life As A Martial Art* (North Atlantic Books, 1991), his private practice focuses on long-standing conditions that resist change. He is currently a professor of Qi Gong (Chinese therapeutic exercise) and T'ai Chi at Five Branches Institute of Chinese Medicine in Santa Cruz, California.